Vegetarian Rice Cuisine

From Pancakes to Paella, 125 Delicious Recipes

Jay Solomon

PRIMA PUBLISHING

*This book is dedicated to Heidi Noggle
and Drew Solomon.*

Library of Congress Cataloging-in-Publication Data

Solomon, Jay.
   Vegetarian rice cuisine : from pancakes to paella, 125 dishes from around the world / Jay Solomon.
     p. cm.
   Includes index.
   ISBN 0-7615-0081-2
   1. Cookery (Rice) 2. Vegetarian cookery. I. Title.
TX809.R5S58   95-21231
641.6'318—dc20   CIP

95 96 97 98 99 AA 10 9 8 7 6 5 4 3 2 1
Printed in the United States of America.

How to Order:

Single copies may be ordered from Prima Publishing, P.O. Box 1260BK, Rocklin, CA 95677; telephone (916) 632-4400. Quantity discounts are also available. On your letterhead, include information concerning the intended use of the books and the number of books you wish to purchase.

Contents

Chapter 3   Side Dishes with Panache   74

**Chapter 4   Rice around the World:
Magnificent Main Entrées   106**

Contents   *v*

Acknowledgments

I would like to thank Georgia Hughes of Prima Publishing for fervently supporting this book. My hand also goes out in gratitude to my friends who share a penchant for good food: Emily Robin, Marilee and Eamonn Murphy, Jessica and Gaby Robin, Sarah Huber, Helena Das, Beth Ryan, Jeannette McGrogan, Tammy Palmer, and Linda and Jon Meyerhoff.

I would like to acknowledge numerous friends who offered encouragement from afar: Robert and Amy Cima, Shaun Buckley, Janet Welch, James Paradiso (and Roseanne), Leslie Sadoff, Freddi Pollack, Rae Tally, and the Robin family from Chappaqua, New York. My immediate and extended family members have been fountains of sage advice: Jesse and Ann Solomon, Gregory Solomon, Lisa Solomon, Margie, Dick, Margaret, and my grandmother, Mary Badia.

I would also like to thank the USA Rice Council, Lundberg Family Farms, Eden Foods, Uncle Ben's, RiceTec (producers of Texmati), and the Healthy Heart Agency of Tompkins County for providing valuable background information about rice.

This is my sixth cookbook; my editors, family, and friends have nurtured every one of them. With each book my enthusiasm for cooking has continued to grow, my vocation has turned to a passion, and my appetite for the world's foods has remained boundless.

Introduction
The World of Rice

Welcome to the new and exciting world of rice cookery. From gumbo to paella and pilaf to pudding, here is a bounty of healthful and enticing international rice dishes. The glorious grain is nutritious, easy to prepare, and amazingly versatile. *Vegetarian Rice Cuisine* celebrates the renaissance of rice.

The culinary possibilities are inspiring. From the stylish Country Garden Paella and Beet Root Risotto to down-home Jay's Vegetable Jambalaya and West African Jollof Rice, *Vegetarian Rice Cuisine* features a cornucopia of nourishing and imaginative dishes. High in flavor, low in fat, and completely meat free, this lean and adventurous rice cuisine forms the centerpiece of a healthy and vibrant lifestyle.

In addition to a plethora of rice suppers, *Vegetarian Rice Cuisine* overflows with savory soups, light salads, and stellar side dishes. There are meals for every occasion, from Risi Minestrone and Miami Rice and Avocado Salad to Pumpkin Pilau, Indonesian Fried Rice, Wild Rice and Pumpkin Pancakes, and much more. For sweet rice treats, a treasure trove of inventive recipes such as Strawberry-Rhubarb Rice Pie, Carrot-Rice Spice Cake, and rice puddings galore ensures that there will be happy endings in store.

Until recently, rice has been underrated, overlooked, and too often poorly cooked. Generations of Americans grew up eating white homogenous rice with a pat of butter on top; rice rarely strayed from its role as uneventful side dish. In today's enlightened kitchen, however, rice has escaped its predictable (and to some, dreary) existence and risen to new epicurean heights.

This resurgence of rice cookery has been encouraged by the rising tide of ethnic flavors stirring up America's melting pot. Immigrants from Thailand, Vietnam, India, the Caribbean, Latin America, and Asia have brought an affinity for rice to the country's table. A plethora of exotic varieties such as basmati, jasmine, Valencia, and sweet rice have been introduced to America's palate.

There also has been an influx of American-grown whole grain rices at the marketplace. The grocer's shelves are filling with brown rice, Wehani, Texmati, black rice, wild rice, and myriad other fancy rices and gourmet rice blends. Consumption of brown rice alone has increased over a hundredfold since the 1970s, and the trend is continuing. Whole grain rice, once a poor man's fate, is now a gourmet's delight.

It is safe to say that most of the planet shares a penchant for rice. In parts of Asia, "to eat" means "to eat rice." In China, the word for rice and food is the same. Rice symbolizes prosperity and goodwill in cultural ceremonies throughout India and Asia. From Japan to Brazil, Indonesia to the Caribbean, and West Africa to Central America, rice is celebrated and enjoyed. Indeed, rice is what much of the world eats for dinner.

Rice: The Healthful Grain

Rice is at the forefront of a heart-smart diet. It is naturally low in fat, sodium, and calories and has zero cholesterol. When combined with vegetables and legumes, a rice meal offers a complete spectrum of nutrients, especially carbohydrates, protein, and fiber. Rice is easy to digest, gluten-free, and a solid source of energy as well as extremely economical. A little rice goes a long way.

Rice is the quintessential starch. In addition to being an excellent source of complex carbohydrates, it contains several essential vitamins, minerals, and protein. Whole grain rices (such as brown rice) have additional fiber, Vitamin E, and other nutrients. Although white rice loses some minerals and fiber in the milling process, almost all of the white rice processed in America is enriched with niacin, thiamine, iron, and often other nutrients. Parboiled rice retains even more valuable nutrients.

The USDA Food Guide Pyramid highlights the valuable role rice plays in a healthful, well-balanced diet. Rice (along with cereal, bread, and pasta) is a valued complex carbohydrate and is part of the foundation of the food pyramid and makes up the largest food group. According to the Food Guide Pyramid, a person should eat six to eleven servings daily from the rice and grain group. (One-half cup of cooked rice equals one serving.)

It has been well established that a lowfat, high-fiber diet rich in vegetables, beans, and fruits can lead to a reduced risk of some cancers and other afflictions. It so happens that rice is a vegetable's best friend; many of the recipes in *Vegetarian Rice Cuisine* combine rice and vegetables (or fruits) on the same plate or in the same bowl.

One of rice's greatest attributes is its affinity for legumes; rice and beans go hand in hand. When rice is combined with either beans, lentils, or split peas, the meal becomes a nutritional powerhouse, loaded with fiber, complete proteins, and complex carbohydrates. In addition, the new rice cuisine taps into a pantry of fresh and dried herbs, copious spices, potent curries, addictive garlic, and all kinds of feisty chiles. With such an appealing entourage of tastes, there is little need for salty, buttery, or meaty flavors.

Secrets for Perfect Rice

Obviously you don't need a culinary degree to cook rice, but there are a few helpful tips for preparing perfect rice. First, when cooking rice on the stove top always start with a large sturdy pot with a tight-fitting lid. Next, it is important to measure the rice and water according to the recipe or package directions. Combine the rice and water in the pot, stir it once, and bring to a boil over high heat. Once boiling, immediately reduce the heat to low and cover the pan with the lid.

Proceed to cook the rice for the recipe's recommended cooking time. *Do not stir the rice while it simmers* nor lift the lid while it cooks (unless you are making risotto). Stirring will induce the grains to stick and clump together, which is probably not what you want (unless you're making an Asian dish). Lifting the lid releases essential steam and moisture. It's okay to peek at the rice and check for doneness one or two minutes before the allotted time elapses—cooking time will vary slightly depending on the age and variety of rice.

When the rice is tender and all of the liquid is absorbed, remove the pot from the heat and fluff the grains with a fork. Let the rice stand (still covered) for five to ten minutes more before serving. The rice will continue to steam and absorb flavors while resting in the pot.

Risotto, on the other hand, lives by its own rules. This classic Italian dish aspires to be creamy and clingy, not fluffy and separate; the grains mesh and meld together. The nature of risotto demands constant stirring of the uncovered pot, allowing grains to absorb almost twice as much water as regular rice. Risotto is also the exclusive province of short-grained rices such as arborio, an Italian rice.

In general, one cup of uncooked white rice requires about two cups of liquid and takes fifteen to twenty minutes to cook; parboiled rice takes slightly longer. One cup of whole grain rice (such as brown rice) requires slightly more water and takes about twice the cooking time as white rice (about forty minutes).

Many of the recipes in *Vegetarian Rice Cuisine* call for cooking rice in the same pan with a mixture of sautéed vegetables. This vegetable mixture—what Italians call *soffritto* and the Spanish call *sofrito*—imparts an essential aromatic flavor to the rice dish. When herbs and spices are added, the flavors expand exponentially, further reducing the need for salty chicken stock, bouillon cubes, butter, cream, and other unwelcome ingredients. Historically, pilaf, pilau, biryani, risotto, and many other classic rice dishes are prepared this way

Other methods for cooking rice involve microwave ovens, rice cookers, pressure cookers, and the conventional oven. Microwaving is an excellent time-saving device and flavor-efficient way to *reheat* a rice dish. However, cooking rice in a microwave oven from scratch takes about the same time as on the stove top.

A rice cooker's advantages include trouble-free cooking and a finished rice that stays warm for a fairly long time in the cooker. Pressure cooking yields a somewhat more compressed rice, but still desirable. Oven baked rice requires slightly more time than stove top cooking but offers more space for large casserole type dishes.

Most of the rice dishes in *Vegetarian Rice Cuisine* are prepared on the stove top or in the oven. As a seasoned restaurant chef, I am most comfortable towering over the stove range and monitoring the moment. If you favor rice cookers, pressure cookers, or ovens, with a little creativity many of these recipes can be tailored to your taste.

I have known some professional chefs to cook their rice like pasta. In other words, the rice is boiled in plenty of water, and when the grains are *al dente*, the rice is drained in a colander and the liquid discarded. Unfortunately, valuable nutrients and flavor go down the drain with the cooking liquid. I don't recommend this method.

Because most of the white rice sold in this country is enriched (and coated) with nutrients, it is not a good idea to soak or rinse the rice before cooking (unless it is Asian sweet rice). By rinsing the rice, you may unintentionally wash away valuable nutrients. Some cultures habitually rinse rice before cooking to remove dust, but most of today's grains are polished and do not require washing. (Some imported rices, which are not always enriched, do require rinsing).

How Rice Is Harvested:
From Paddy to Pantry

Rice is a water-loving plant grown in flooded fields or rice "paddies." Rice thrives in this aquatic environment, while most weeds do not. When the "rough rice" or "paddy rice" is harvested, it is sent to a mill for processing. At the mill, the bulk of rice's inedible outer hulls (or husks) are removed. At this stage the beige bran layers covering the rice kernels are still intact; the grain is now called brown rice or whole grain rice.

Rice can remain as brown rice or continue to be processed into white rice (or polished rice). For white rice, the outer bran layers are removed from the grains, leaving white kernels. Often the rice is then polished and enriched with thiamine, niacin, and iron, replacing some of the nutrients lost in the milling process. The bulk of the world's rice is polished and enriched. The rice is now ready for the market. (However, some rices, such as Indian basmati, are aged for several years to acquire a stronger flavor.)

Parboiled rice undergoes a slightly different milling process. The rough rice is soaked first in water, steamed under pressure, and dried before milling. This procedure drives nutrients into the grain and results in less mineral erosion during the milling process. In addition, parboiled rice is fluffy and remains separate when cooked. Uncle Ben's trademark "converted rice" is parboiled. Despite its name, parboiled rice is not "precooked" rice; it actually takes slightly longer to cook than regular milled rice.

Once the rice has been transported from the grocery store to your home, it should be stored in a cool, dry pantry. Unopened white rice should keep indefinitely. Brown rice, because of its bran content, has a shorter shelf life and should keep for about six months. If your brown rice is not used frequently, store it in the refrigerator. Once opened, all rices should be tightly covered. Cooked rice dishes, if well covered and refrigerated, should keep for five to six days.

A Brief Scientific Interlude

Whether a rice is fluffy or sticky depends a great deal on its physical properties. Every kind of rice is composed of two major types of starch, amylose, and amylopectin. The ratio of amylose and amylopectin in the grain determines the textural qualities of rice when it is cooked, that is, how fluffy or sticky it will be.

Amylopectin is a more readily released starch when cooked in liquid than amylose; it gels more easily. It follows that short grain rice—which is high in amylopectin—is waxy and sticky when cooked. Long grain rice—which has a higher amount of amylose and a lower amount of amylopectin—cooks up fluffy and separate. Arborio, the short grain rice that gives risotto its creamy texture, is high in amylopectin. Basmati, which is light and fluffy, is high in amylose.

Rice: A Historical Perspective

Rice has fed the world for centuries and is believed to be one of the earliest known harvested crops. Many refer to China as the cradle of rice's cultivation, tracing the grain as far back as an emperor's ceremony for a rice planting around 2800 B.C. Over several centuries, rice spread throughout Asia, ancient Persia and Greece, the Middle East, Africa, Europe, and on to the Americas.

Rice first came to this country's shores in the mid-seventeenth century. It didn't flourish as a crop until just before the eighteenth century when a ship from West Africa arrived in Charleston, South Carolina, with "Golde Seede Rice." This breed of rice thrived in the South, and the Carolinas eventually became a major grower and exporter of "Carolina Gold." In the mid-1800s the Civil War wiped out much of the region's rice industry, and production moved westward to Louisiana, Texas, Arkansas, Mississippi, and Missouri.

By the twentieth century the arrival of mechanized planting and harvesting accelerated the expansion of rice production on the Gulf Coast and West Coast. California, buoyed by a large influx of Asians, soon joined the ranks of major rice growers. As rice became a fixture on the American menu, growers kept up with demand; according to the USA Rice Council, 90 percent of all rice consumed in this country is homegrown. Americans eat twice as much rice today as they did a decade ago.

The consumption of wild rice also has increased dramatically in recent years. In the botanical sense, wild rice is not really a rice, but a seed of an aquatic water-loving grass. Wild rice flourishes in northern lakes and rivers throughout Minnesota and Canada; in fact, it is the only native grain grown in North America. Legend has it that American Indians harvested the "free range" rice by paddling their canoes between vegetation and shaking the plants, catching the rice in their canoes. Much of today's wild rice is raised in man-made paddies, but the grains still retain their earthy, grassy character.

In short, there has never been a better time to appreciate the abundant virtues of rice cookery. As a chef, teacher, and rice epicure, I invite you to share in the bountiful pleasures of *Vegetarian Rice Cuisine*.

Jay Solomon

Ithaca, New York

A Glossary
of Rice

It is important to note that rice is referred to by both the size and the variety of the grain. Although there are hundreds of varieties of rice, there are only three common sizes. Here is a description of each size.

Long grain rice is three or more times as long as it is wide. When cooked, the grains become fluffy and remain separate. Basmati and much of the white rice sold in America is long grain rice.

Medium grain rice is two to three times as long as it is wide. When cooked, medium grains stick together slightly more than long grain rice but not as much as short grain rice. Valencia is a medium grain rice.

Short grain rice is short and plump; the length is less than twice its width. When cooked, short grain rice sticks together more than long grain or medium grain and exhibits a creamy, softer consistency. Arborio and sticky rice are short grained.

Here is a descriptive guide to common and exotic rices.

Arborio: This is a cherished Italian rice. The pearly white grains develop a soft, creamy consistency when cooked. Arborio is perfect for risotto, soup, and pudding.

Aromatic Rice: This term refers to a family of rices that have a nutty flavor and roasted popcornlike aroma. The grains tend to be long and slender. Varieties include basmati, jasmine, Texmati, Jasmati, wild pecan, and Uncle Ben's Aromatica.

Basmati: The name literally means "queen of fragrance." Basmati is an aromatic, nutty long grain rice native to

India and Pakistan. When cooked, the grains become slender and fluffy. Basmati is now being grown in the United States; brown basmati is also available.

Black Rice: This exotic blackish purple medium or short grain rice is popular in Southeast Asian cuisine. Black rice is available in well-stocked Asian markets and in whole grain rice blends. Lundberg Family Farms of California sells a black japonica rice blend that is a combination of black rice and a russet-colored rice.

Brown Rice: This whole grain rice still has its outer bran layer intact. Brown rice has a nutty flavor, chewy texture, and beige color. It has twice the fiber of polished white rice. Brown rice takes about thirty-five to forty minutes to cook; one cup of uncooked rice requires 2 1/4 to 2 1/2 cups liquid. Brown rice can be short, medium, or long grained.

Glutinous Rice: *See* Sweet Rice.

Instant Rice: This is also called precooked rice or quick-cooking rice. This rice has been milled, completely cooked, and then dehydrated and enriched. While it cooks in just a few minutes, it loses much of its personality somewhere along the line. It should not be confused with parboiled rice, which is not precooked.

Jasmati: This long grain white American rice shares the aromatic nature and soft texture of Thai jasmine rice. It is marketed with the Texmati brands.

Jasmine Rice: This fragrant, nutty, silken long grain white rice has a delicate popcornlike aroma (similar to basmati). When cooked the grains become moist, sticky, and delectable. Jasmine rice is native to Thailand and is also called Thai Fragrant. It takes twelve to fifteen minutes to cook.

Kasmati: An aromatic, white basmati-style rice grown in the United States and marketed with the Texmati brands. Like basmati, its grains become fluffy and slender when cooked. It can be used interchangeably with basmati in most dishes.

Parboiled Rice: This also is called "converted" rice, which is Uncle Ben's trademark. Before milling, the whole rice is soaked in water, pressurized, steamed, and then dried. This treatment saves some nutrients in the milling process. Parboiled rice yields fluffy grains that remain separate when cooked. The rice takes slightly longer to cook than regularly milled rice and requires slightly more liquid. It can be used interchangeably with long grain white rice in most recipes.

Riz Cous: These are broken grains of brown rice marketed by Lundberg Family Farms. The rice is a cross between couscous and light brown rice and can be used in place of couscous.

Sweet Rice: Also called glutinous, sticky, or waxy rice. Although it is not overtly sweet, this rice becomes sticky, soft, and gelatinous when cooked. It makes an ideal ingredient for pastry fillings, puddings, Asian desserts, and sushi. Most sweet rices are soaked in water for several hours before steaming or cooking.

Texmati: This refers to a variety of American aromatic rices including white long grain, brown, and light brown (which has been partially milled). White Texmati rice is a cross between basmati and long grain rice.

Valencia: This rice is named for the region in Spain where it is grown. Valencia has a medium, pearly white grain and is the traditional rice for paella. It is sometimes used in place of arborio rice.

Wehani: This mahogany-colored aromatic whole grain rice is marketed by Lundberg Family Farms in California. It has a robust, nutty flavor and takes forty to forty-five minutes to cook. Cook one cup of Wehani in 2¼ to 2½ cups liquid.

White Long Grain Rice: This is one of the most widely available rices. The outer bran layer of the grain has been removed in the milling process, leaving a polished white grain. Some nutrients are lost in the process, but the rice is later enriched. Long grain white rice cooks in about fifteen minutes; cook one cup of rice in about two cups of liquid.

Whole Grain Rice Blends: There are a growing number of gourmet "rice blends" on the market. Whole grain rice blends often include brown rice, wild rice, and black rice.

Wild Pecan: This long grain aromatic rice has a nutty aroma and pecanlike flavor, but contains neither wild rice nor pecans. It is grown in Louisiana country and is a staple of Cajun cooking. Konriko is the major brand.

Wild Rice: Botanically speaking, wild rice is not really a rice but the dark seed of a native North American aquatic grass. The grain is firm and chewy and has an earthy, grassy flavor. Wild rice takes forty-five to fifty minutes; cook one cup of wild rice in about three cups of liquid. It is predominantly grown in Minnesota and Canada. Wild rice is often blended with whole grain rices.

Chapter 1

Savory Rice
Soup Meals

Rice fortifies a variety of soups, chilies, chowders, and gumbos. The grain adds body and substance to the soup kettle while soaking up and spreading a soup's brothy flavors. These soups serve as a splendid first course, or if you are in the mood for something light, a rice soup needs only fresh bread and a tossed salad for a satisfying whole meal.

In this brand of rice-inspired soup cookery, the grain turns up in unexpected places. From Beet and Rice Borscht, Wintry White Bean and Rice Chili, and Mexican Corn and Rice Soup to Rice Pot-au-Feu and Three Grain–Three Mushroom Soup, rice delights and surprises the senses. From the mellifluous Risi Minestrone to the piquant Good-for-You Gumbo, these soups offer a ladle of nourishment in a bowl. In addition, a little goes a long way as rice expands several times in volume when cooked.

Although all kinds of rice are welcome in the soup kitchen, here are a few helpful tips. For longer-cooking soups I prefer to use brown rice or other whole grain rice; the durable grain appreciates the lengthy cooking time. Short grain rice is a natural favorite for thick soups, chowders, and bisques. And for some soup presentations, such as gumbo and Indian mulligatawny, the rice is cooked separately and added near the finish or placed in the bowl before adding the soup.

Beet and Rice Borscht

"This is not your grandmother's borscht," I repeated as I ladled out this magenta-hued soup at a dinner party. Indeed, this alluring beet and rice combination proved to be a sure-fire winner that night, silencing memories of borscht past. Many asked for the recipe, thank you very much.

1	tablespoon olive oil
1	medium red onion, diced
1	small zucchini, diced
3	or 4 cloves garlic, minced
2	or 3 large beets, scrubbed and diced (about 2 cups)
1	large white potato, diced
6	cups hot water
1	tablespoon dried oregano
2	teaspoons dried basil
1	teaspoon salt
1/2	teaspoon ground black pepper
1/2	cup arborio rice or other short grain white rice
1/4	cup canned tomato paste
1	(15-ounce) can red kidney beans, drained
2	cups chopped escarole or beet greens (optional)

Heat the oil in a large saucepan and add the onion, zucchini, and garlic. Sauté for 5 to 7 minutes. Add the beets, potato, water, and seasonings and cook for 20 minutes over low-medium heat, stirring occasionally. Stir in the rice and tomato paste and cook for 20 to 25 minutes more, stirring occasionally, until the rice and beets are tender. Stir in the beans and greens and simmer for 5 to 10 minutes more.

Let the soup stand for 10 minutes. If you'd like, puree the soup in a blender or food processor fitted with a steel blade before serving. Offer lowfat plain yogurt as a topping.

Yield: 8 servings

Rice Advice

When in season, add 2 or 3 tablespoons chopped fresh dill or basil to the soup a few minutes before serving.

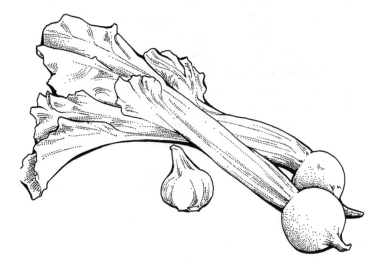

Good-for-You Gumbo

It is said that in most parts of the world, people eat to live. In Louisiana, people live to eat. Gumbo exemplifies the spirit and gusto of Louisiana cooking. This meat-free, healthful version is filled with harvest vegetables and zesty spices. Gumbo is always served over a bowl of steaming rice. (The word gumbo *comes from an African word for "okra").*

1 1/2 tablespoons canola oil
1   medium yellow onion, diced
1   yellow or red bell pepper, seeded and diced
2   cups diced eggplant
2   or 3 cloves garlic, minced
6   cups hot water
1   (14-ounce) can stewed tomatoes
2   medium carrots, peeled and diced
1   cup chopped okra, fresh or frozen
2   teaspoons dried oregano
1 1/2 teaspoons dried thyme
1/2   teaspoon ground black pepper
1/8   to 1/2 teaspoon ground cayenne pepper
1   teaspoon salt
4   to 6 cups cooked white or brown rice, heated
       Fresh scallions, chives, or parsley (optional garnish)

Heat the oil in a large saucepan and add the onion, bell pepper, eggplant, and garlic. Cook for 8 to 10 minutes over medium heat, stirring frequently. Stir in the water, tomatoes, carrots, okra, and seasonings and cook over low heat for 30 to 40 minutes, stirring occasionally.

Place about 1/2 cup of the cooked rice in the bottom of each soup bowl. Ladle the gumbo over the rice. If you'd like, top with chopped scallions, chives, or parsley.

Yield: 8 servings

Rice Advice

Make sure there is a bottle of red-hot sauce or Tabasco on the table for last minute spicing! To make this a soup supper, add 1 (15-ounce) can of red kidney beans or black-eyed peas to the broth near the end of the cooking phase.

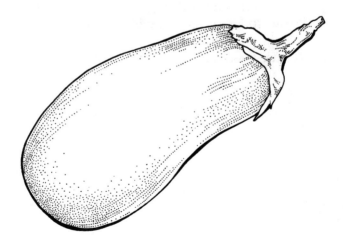

Black Bean and Brown Rice Chili

Chili is the ultimate cold-weather comfort food. Having endured many long, blustery winters in my life, I have become a connoisseur of homemade chili. This "bowl of red" is highly spiced, chunky with vegetables, and munificent with flavor.

1/2	cup brown rice
1	cup hot water
1	tablespoon canola oil
1	medium red onion, diced
1	green bell pepper, seeded and diced
2	stalks celery, chopped
2	cloves garlic, minced
1	(16-ounce) can crushed tomatoes (about 2 cups)
1	(15-ounce) can black beans, drained
1	tablespoon chili powder
1	tablespoon dried oregano
1 1/2	teaspoons ground cumin
1/2	teaspoon ground black pepper
1/2	teaspoon salt

Combine the rice and hot water in a saucepan and bring to a boil. Cover and cook for 35 to 40 minutes over low heat until all of the liquid is absorbed. Fluff the rice and let stand for 5 to 10 minutes.

Meanwhile, heat the oil in a saucepan and add the onion, bell pepper, celery, and garlic. Cook for 7 to 9 minutes over medium heat, stirring frequently. Stir in the crushed tomatoes, beans, and seasonings and cook for 10 minutes over low heat, stirring occasionally. Stir in the rice and cook for 10 to 15 minutes more. Ladle the chili into bowls and serve hot. Pass a bottle of Tabasco or other hot sauce at the table. Serve with corn bread.

Yield: 4 servings

Spicy Dal and Rice Soup

Some soups, by the nature of their ingredients, exude good-ness and well-being. This curried broth of lentils, rice, and potatoes is both nourishing and comforting. If you have a penchant for vibrant, earthy curry flavors, this soup will surely satisfy.

1	tablespoon canola oil
1	medium red onion, chopped
1	green or red bell pepper, seeded and diced
2	cloves garlic, minced
1	or 2 jalapeño peppers or other chile, seeded and minced
2	tomatoes, diced
2	teaspoons curry powder (Madras style, if possible)
1	teaspoon ground cumin
1/2	teaspoon ground turmeric
1/2	teaspoon ground black pepper
6	cups hot water
1	cup green lentils, rinsed
1/2	cup brown rice or white rice*
2	medium red or white potatoes, diced
3/4	teaspoon salt

* If using white rice, add to the soup along with the potatoes.

Heat the oil in a saucepan and add the onion, bell pepper, garlic, and jalapeños. Sauté for 5 minutes. Stir in the tomatoes and seasonings (except the salt) and cook for 1 minute more over low-medium heat. Stir in the water, lentils, and brown rice and cook for about 15 minutes, stirring occasionally. Stir in the potatoes and cook for 30 to 40 minutes more until the lentils are tender.

Stir in the salt right before serving. Serve with a warm flat bread such as chapati, nan, or pita bread.

Yield: 8 servings

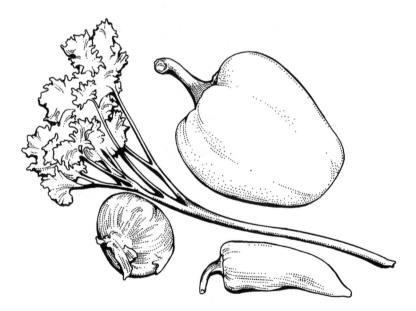

Risi Minestrone

Although minestrone is traditionally prepared with pasta, rice offers a refreshing change of pace, and it works. This hearty vegetable and rice soup will woo even the most ardent pasta lover away from the squiggly noodles.

1	tablespoon olive oil
1	small yellow onion, diced
2	cups chopped leeks
1	small zucchini, diced
8	to 12 mushrooms, sliced
2	cloves garlic, minced
6	cups hot water
1/2	cup arborio or other short grain white rice
1	(14-ounce) can stewed tomatoes
1	medium white potato, diced
1/4	cup tomato paste
1	tablespoon dried oregano
2	teaspoons dried basil
3/4	teaspoon salt
1/2	teaspoon ground black pepper

Vegetarian Rice Cuisine

Heat the oil in a large saucepan and add the onion, leeks, zucchini, mushrooms, and garlic. Cook over medium heat for 8 to 10 minutes, stirring frequently. Stir in the water, rice, stewed tomatoes, potato, tomato paste, and seasonings and bring to a simmer. Cook for about 30 minutes over low-medium heat, stirring occasionally. Remove from the heat and let stand for several minutes. Ladle the minestrone into bowls and serve with warm Italian bread.

Yield: 8 servings

Rice Advice

If fresh herbs are in season, add a few tablespoons of chopped basil, oregano, or arugula to the soup near the end of the cooking time.

Native Pumpkin and Wild Rice Soup

This soup offers a trio of tastes: the delicate flavor of pumpkin, the strong earthiness of wild rice, and the fragrant essence of herbs. Either sugar pie pumpkin, West Indian pumpkin, or butternut squash may be used in the soup.

1/2	cup wild rice
1 1/2	cups hot water
1	tablespoon canola oil
1	medium yellow onion, diced
1	green bell pepper, seeded and diced
2	cloves garlic, minced
6	cups water
2	cups peeled, diced pumpkin or other winter squash
2	tablespoons dried parsley (or 1/4 cup chopped fresh)
1	teaspoon dried oregano
1	teaspoon dried thyme leaves
1	teaspoon ground cumin
1	teaspoon salt
1/2	teaspoon ground black pepper

Combine the wild rice and hot water in a saucepan and cover. Cook over low-medium heat for 40 to 45 minutes until the rice is tender. Fluff and set aside.

Heat the oil in another saucepan and add the onion, bell pepper, and garlic. Sauté for 5 to 7 minutes. Add the water, pumpkin, and seasonings and cook for 15 minutes over medium heat, stirring occasionally. Stir in the cooked rice and cook for 10 to 15 minutes more over low heat, stirring occasionally.

Ladle the soup into bowls and serve hot.

Yield: 6 servings

Rice Advice

For a hotter version, add 1 jalapeño pepper (seeded and minced) with the garlic and other vegetables. If wild rice is not available, try long grain brown rice, Wehani, or basmati.

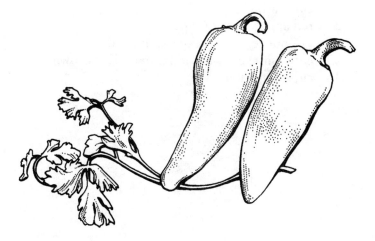

Root Vegetable Mulligatawny

This chunky Indian soup has a kaleidoscope of intense flavors and textures; parsnips, potatoes, and apples float unmoored in the broth. Mulligatawny, which means "pepper water," is an Indian version of gumbo. This version is fruitier than most.

1	tablespoon canola oil
1	medium yellow onion, diced
1	green bell pepper, seeded and diced
1	large tomato, diced
2	teaspoons minced fresh ginger
2 1/2	teaspoons curry powder
1 1/2	teaspoons ground cumin
1	teaspoon salt
1/4	teaspoon ground cayenne pepper
6	cups water
1	large parsnip, peeled and diced
1	medium white potato, diced
1/2	cup raisins
2	red apples, diced (unpeeled)
1	(15-ounce) can chickpeas, drained
2	cups white basmati or Texmati light brown rice
4	cups hot water

Heat the oil in a large saucepan and add the onion, bell pepper, tomato, and ginger. Sauté for 5 to 7 minutes. Add the seasonings and sauté for 1 minute more. Stir in the water, parsnip, potato, and raisins and cook over low-medium heat for about 15 minutes, stirring occasionally. Stir in the apples and cook for 20 minutes more. Stir in the chickpeas and cook for 5 to 10 minutes more.

Meanwhile, combine the rice and hot water in a saucepan and bring to a boil. Cover and cook for 15 to 20 minutes over low heat, until the rice is tender. Fluff the rice and let stand for 5 to 10 minutes.

When the soup is ready to serve, spoon the rice into soup bowls and ladle the mulligatawny over the top. Serve with Indian flat bread or pita bread.

Yield: 6 to 8 servings

Miso Rice Soup

Miso is a nutrient-rich soy bean paste favored in Japanese cooking. It instills a deep sealike flavor and dark tint to this brothy, rice-enriched soup. The steaming soup is topped with raw vegetables, an enlightened combination.

1	tablespoon canola oil
1	medium yellow onion, finely chopped
2	large carrots, peeled and diced
2	cloves garlic, minced
6	cups water
2	or 3 strips kombu (edible seaweed), soaked in water and diced
4	scallions, chopped
1	2-inch section of daikon, peeled and sliced thin
1/3	cup sweet white rice or other short grain rice
2	to 3 tablespoons miso paste
2	to 3 tablespoons warm water
1	cup bean sprouts
	Salt and black pepper, to taste

Heat the oil in a large saucepan and add the onion, carrots, and garlic. Cook over medium heat for 5 to 7 minutes, stirring frequently. Add the water, kombu, half of the scallions and daikon and bring to a boil. Cook over low heat for about 5 minutes. Add the rice and cook for about 20 to 30 minutes until the rice is tender.

Meanwhile, dissolve the miso paste in the warm water. When the rice has finished cooking, stir the miso into the soup. Do not boil the soup once the miso paste has been added.

Ladle the soup into large soup bowls and top with the bean sprouts and the remaining scallions. Season with salt and pepper at the table.

Yield: 6 servings

Rice Advice

Miso can be found in Asian markets and near the soy sauce in well-stocked grocery stores. Kombu is an edible seaweed that comes to life when steeped in a soupy broth. Kombu is available in Japanese and Asian markets, as well as well-stocked natural food stores.

Sante Fe Posole Stew

Posole is the Southwestern equivalent of Tex-Mex chili. The main ingredient is hominy, a chewy corn that has been dried, preserved, and rehydrated. Like a good homemade chili, posole satisfies a longing for wholesome, unpretentious comfort food.

1/2	cup long grain white rice
1	cup hot water
1	tablespoon canola oil
1	medium yellow onion, diced
1	red or green bell pepper, seeded and diced
2	cloves garlic, minced
1	jalapeño pepper, seeded and minced
1	(16-ounce) can crushed tomatoes
1	(15-ounce) can hominy, drained
1	cup cooked or canned black beans or red kidney beans
1	cup water
2	tablespoons dried parsley
2	teaspoons dried oregano
1 1/2	teaspoons ground cumin
1/2	teaspoon salt
1/4	teaspoon ground black pepper
	Chopped fresh cilantro or shredded lowfat cheese (optional garnish)

Combine the rice and hot water in a saucepan and bring to a boil. Cover and cook for about 15 minutes over low heat. Fluff the rice and remove from the heat.

Heat the oil in a large saucepan and add the onion, bell pepper, garlic, and jalapeño. Sauté for about 5 minutes. Stir in the cooked rice, crushed tomatoes, hominy, beans, water, and seasonings. Cook for about 15 minutes over low heat, stirring occasionally.

Ladle into bowls and serve with warm flour tortillas. If you'd like, top the posole with chopped fresh cilantro or shredded lowfat cheese.

Yield: 4 to 6 servings

Rice Advice

Hominy is available canned in most well-stocked grocery stores.

Wintry White Bean and Rice Chili

This healthful vegetable kettle is a "two fisted meal"—hold a hunk of bread in one hand, a large soupspoon in the other, and go for it. Tell your guests to come to the table with an appetite.

1 tablespoon canola oil
1 medium yellow onion, diced
1 green bell pepper, seeded and diced
2 stalks celery, diced
2 cloves garlic, minced
1 (15-ounce) can white kidney beans (cannelini), drained
1 (14-ounce) can stewed tomatoes
1 1/2 cups hot water
3/4 cup long grain white rice
2 tablespoons tomato paste
1 1/2 tablespoons chili powder
1 tablespoon dried oregano
1 1/2 teaspoons ground cumin
1/2 teaspoon ground black pepper
1/2 teaspoon salt

Heat the oil in a saucepan and add the onion, bell pepper, celery, and garlic. Cook for 7 to 9 minutes over medium heat, stirring frequently. Stir in the beans, stewed tomatoes, water, rice, tomato paste, and seasonings and bring to a boil. Cover and cook for about 25 minutes over low heat, stirring occasionally. Let stand for 10 minutes before serving.

Ladle the chili into bowls and serve with fresh bread and a tossed salad.

Yield: 4 servings

Rice Advice

Pass the Tabasco or another bottled hot sauce at the table. (What would chili be without Tabasco?) You can also top the chili with shredded lowfat cheese.

Sweet Potato Risotto Chowder

The Italian kitchen intersects with the American Southwest for this luscious cauldron of rice and vegetables. Although many chowders are made with fat-laden heavy cream, this version relies on creamy arborio rice and potatoes for thickening.

1	tablespoon canola oil
1	medium red onion, chopped
1	red bell pepper, seeded and diced
2	or 3 cloves garlic, minced
6	cups hot water
2	medium sweet potatoes, diced (about 2 cups)
1/2	cup arborio rice
2	tablespoons chopped fresh parsley (or 1 tablespoon dried)
1	teaspoon dried oregano
1	teaspoon paprika
1/2	teaspoon salt
1/2	teaspoon ground black pepper
1	cup corn kernels, fresh or frozen
1/4	to 1/2 cup grated Parmesan cheese

Heat the oil in the saucepan and add the onion, bell pepper, and garlic. Sauté for 5 to 7 minutes. Add the water, potatoes, rice, and seasonings and cook over low-medium heat for 30 to 40 minutes, stirring occasionally. Stir in the corn and continue cooking for 20 to 30 minutes more, stirring occasionally.

Remove from the heat and blend in the Parmesan cheese. Ladle the chowder into bowls and serve with warm bread.

Yield: 8 servings

Brown Rice and Squash Pepperpot

Pepperpot is a spicy Pan-Caribbean soup prepared with a variety of ingredients, including squash, rice, hardy vegetables, and chiles. I've left out the meat and doubled up on squash and kale, two items loaded with healthful antioxidants.

1	tablespoon canola oil
1	medium yellow onion, diced
1	large green or red bell pepper, seeded and diced
2	cloves garlic, minced
1	or 2 jalapeño or Red Fresno peppers or 1/2 Scotch bonnet pepper, seeded and minced
6	cups hot water
2	cups peeled, diced butternut or hubbard squash
2	medium carrots, peeled and diced
1/2	cup short grain or medium grain brown rice
2	tablespoons dried parsley
1	teaspoon dried thyme
1/2	teaspoon ground black pepper
1/2	teaspoon salt
1/4	teaspoon ground turmeric
2	cups chopped kale or spinach

In a large saucepan, heat the oil and add the onion, bell pepper, garlic, and chile(s). Sauté for about 5 minutes. Add the water, squash, carrots, rice, and seasonings and cook for 40 minutes over low heat, stirring occasionally. Stir in the kale and cook for 5 to 10 minutes more.

Let the soup stand for 5 to 10 minutes before serving. Ladle into bowls and serve hot.

Yield: 6 servings

Mexican Corn and Rice Soup

Chiles light up the skyline of Mexican cooking with a warm glow. Chipotle, serrano, ancho, jalapeño, and myriad others provide a fiesta of penetrating sensations. This South-of-the-Border soup demonstrates how chiles (when used judiciously) can heighten and enhance (and romance) the palate.

1	tablespoon canola oil
1	medium yellow onion, diced
1	small zucchini, diced
1	green or red bell pepper, seeded and diced
2	or 3 cloves garlic, minced
1	chipotle, jalapeño pepper, or other hot chile, seeded and minced
6	cups water
2	cups chopped kale, escarole, or Swiss chard
2	plum tomatoes, diced
1/2	cup short grain or medium grain white rice
2	teaspoons dried oregano
1 1/2	teaspoons ground cumin
3/4	teaspoon salt
2	cups corn kernels, fresh or frozen

Heat the oil in a large saucepan and add the onion, zucchini, bell pepper, garlic, and chile. Sauté for 5 to 7 minutes. Add the water, kale, tomatoes, rice, and seasonings and bring to a boil. Reduce the heat to low and cook for about 20 minutes, stirring occasionally. Stir in the corn and simmer for 10 to 15 minutes more.

Let the soup stand for a few minutes before serving. Ladle into bowls and serve with warm flour tortillas.

Yield: 6 to 8 servings

Rice Advice

Sprinkle shredded Monterey jack cheese over the soup right before serving. For an authentic herbal touch, blend in 2 or 3 tablespoons of chopped fresh cilantro or epazote when you add the corn. Roasting a poblano chile and adding it to the soup is another viable option.

Italian Tomato and Bread Bisque

In Boston for a First Night celebration, I stumbled into a neighborhood tavern (Spazzo's) to escape the cold. At the bar we ordered pappa al pomodoro, an appetizing, herb-scented tomato and garlic soup. Bread is tossed in at the last minute and left to soak up the delectable flavors. It was a fortuitous way to start the New Year. Here is my re-created winter version.

4	or 5 slices dark bread or Italian bread, cut into bite-size pieces
2	tablespoons olive oil
1	medium yellow onion, diced
2	large cloves garlic, minced
1	(28-ounce) can stewed tomatoes
2	teaspoons dried oregano
2	teaspoons dried basil
3/4	teaspoon salt
1/2	teaspoon ground black pepper
3	cups hot water
1/3	cup arborio or other short grain white rice
10	fresh basil or arugula leaves, coarsely chopped

Preheat the oven to 350° F.

Spread the bread out on a baking sheet. Place in the oven and bake for 10 to 15 minutes, until lightly toasted. Set aside and let cool.

Heat the oil in a large saucepan and add the onion and garlic. Sauté for 4 minutes. Stir in the stewed tomatoes and dried seasonings and cook for about 5 minutes over medium heat, stirring frequently. Stir in the water and rice and bring to a boil. Cook for about 25 minutes over low heat, stirring occasionally. Remove from the heat and let cool slightly.

Transfer the soup to a food processor fitted with a steel blade or to a blender. Process for about 10 seconds, until creamy. Return to the pan and stir in the bread and fresh basil. Ladle into bowls and serve hot.

Yield: 4 servings

Rice Advice
Pass a little grated Parmesan cheese at the table.

Split-Pea, Carrot, and Rice Potage

A split-pea soup should have a fluid, thick texture (not crunchy), and the vegetables should have a melt-in-your-mouth (but never mushy) tenderness. Ham or bacon should be nowhere in sight. A friend of mine, Eamonn Murphy, who makes a salubrious split-pea soup, inspired this recipe.

1	tablespoon canola oil
1	medium red onion, diced
1	green or red bell pepper, seeded and diced
2	stalks celery, chopped
2	cloves garlic, minced
8	cups water
3/4	cup yellow or green split peas, rinsed
2	tablespoons dried parsley
3/4	teaspoon ground black pepper
1/4	teaspoon ground turmeric
2	cups peeled, diced carrots, or butternut or hubbard squash
1/2	cup white rice or brown rice*
2	cups chopped fresh spinach, Swiss chard, or red kale
1	teaspoon salt

* If using brown rice, add at the start with the split peas and water.

Heat the oil in a saucepan and add the onion, bell pepper, celery, and garlic. Sauté for 5 to 7 minutes. Stir in the water, split peas, and seasonings (except the salt) and cook for 30 minutes over low-medium heat, stirring occasionally. Stir in the carrots and rice and cook for about 20 to 30 minutes more, until the split peas and carrots are tender. Stir in the greens and salt and cook for 5 to 10 minutes more over low heat.

Serve the soup with warm hearth-style bread.

Yield: 6 to 8 servings

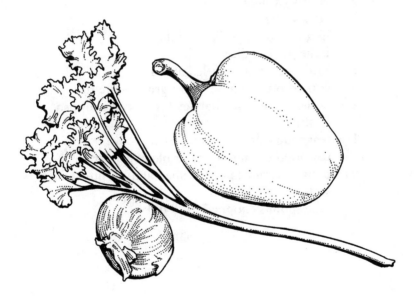

Rice Pot-au-Feu

When I think of pot-au-feu (which means "pot on the fire" in French), I envision this wholesome cauldron of simmering root vegetables, potatoes, rice, and herbs. Give me a bowl of this soup, a hunk of bread, and a little elbowroom and I will be quite content.

1	tablespoon canola oil
1	medium yellow onion, diced
2	cups chopped leeks
1	stalk celery, chopped
2	cloves garlic, minced
6	cups water
1	large parsnip, peeled and diced
1	large potato, diced
2	medium carrots, peeled and diced
1/3	cup arborio or other short grain white rice
2	tablespoons dried parsley (or 1/4 cup chopped fresh)
1	teaspoon salt
1/2	teaspoon ground white or black pepper
1/4	pound green beans, trimmed and cut into 1-inch sections
2	tablespoons chopped fresh dill

In a large saucepan, heat the oil and add the onion, leeks, celery, and garlic. Sauté for about 5 minutes. Add the water, parsnip, potato, carrots, rice, and dried seasonings and cook for 25 to 30 minutes over low heat, stirring occasionally, until the vegetables are tender. Stir in the green beans and dill and cook for 5 to 10 minutes more.

Let the soup stand for a few minutes before serving. Ladle into bowls and serve with warm dark bread or French bread.

Yield: 6 servings

Rice Advice

Make this *soupe au pistou* by swirling one or two table-spoons of Arugula Basil Pesto (page 174) or Spinach Pesto (page 173) into the soup at the table. Also, most leeks require a thorough rinsing before chopping.

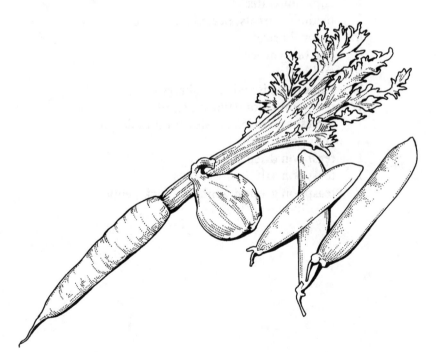

Three Grain–Three Mushroom Soup

Talk about pleasures of the table! This exultant multigrain soup is imbued with the woodsy, buttery flavors of a tasty trio of mushrooms. The whole mushroom genre has expanded immensely in recent years and a variety of both dried and fresh specimens are widely available.

1	tablespoon canola oil
8	ounces button mushrooms, sliced
8	to 10 fresh shiitake mushrooms, sliced
3	medium fresh oyster mushrooms, sliced
1	medium yellow onion, diced
2	cloves garlic, minced
7	cups hot water
2	medium carrots, peeled and diced
1/4	cup wild rice
1/4	cup brown rice
1/4	cup barley
1/4	cup dry white wine or sherry
1	teaspoon Dijon-style mustard
1	tablespoon dried parsley (or 2 tablespoons chopped fresh)
1	teaspoon dried thyme
1	teaspoon salt
1/2	teaspoon ground white or black pepper

In a large saucepan, heat the oil and add the mushrooms, onion, and garlic. Cook for 8 to 10 minutes over medium heat, stirring frequently. Add the water, carrots, both rices, barley, wine, mustard, and seasonings. Cook for 50 minutes to 1 hour over low heat, stirring occasionally.

Let the soup stand for several minutes before serving. Ladle into bowls and serve with dark bread.

Yield: 6 servings

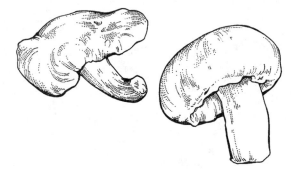

Chapter 2
Entice with Rice
Sumptuous Salads

Rice salads are versatile, healthful, and easy to prepare. You can serve a rice salad as a palate-stimulating first course, an appetizing lunch, or a light dinner entrée. In addition, rice offers diversity in a course that is too often dominated by pasta and potato salad.

Like pasta, rice benefits from refreshing vinaigrettes and sprightly dressings. The optimal dressing for a rice salad is a light blend of oil and vinegar or citrus juice. A variety of fresh and dried herbs, garlic, ginger, and fresh chiles provide penetrating flavors. Fresh parsley, mint, or cilantro is always welcome. A bounty of seasonal vegetables, beans, and lentils fill up the salad bowl.

Once the rice salad is assembled and tossed together, it should be refrigerated for about 1 hour to allow the flavors to mingle and meld together. When ready, fluff the rice salad and serve on a bed of leafy lettuce. Garnish with herbs or vegetables.

Without a doubt, long grain rice makes the best salads. The fluffier and lighter the grain, the more likely the salad will retain a certain liveliness and *esprit*. Another salad strategy calls for mixing and matching two or more rices or other grains. For instance, when wild rice or brown rice is added to a white rice salad, the whole personality changes (for the better, of course).

If possible, use fresh cooked rice for a salad (as opposed to leftover rice). Any decline in quality of the rice while it is stored in the refrigerator will be magnified in the salad. (Leftover rice is good for fried rices and other cooked dishes.)

Mediterranean Herb and Rice Salad

A trio of Mediterranean herbs—mint, oregano, and thyme— brightens and enlivens this melange of rice and vegetables.

3	tablespoons olive oil
2	tablespoons red wine vinegar or balsamic vinegar
1	teaspoon Dijon-style mustard
1/4	cup chopped fresh mint leaves (or 1 1/2 table-spoons dried)
1	tablespoon fresh oregano (2 teaspoons dried)
1	teaspoon dried thyme leaves
1/2	teaspoon ground black pepper
4	cups cooked long grain white rice or brown rice
2	tomatoes, diced
3	or 4 scallions, chopped
1	small cucumber, diced
2	cloves garlic, minced
1	cup pitted medium black olives, sliced
1	(15-ounce) can chickpeas, drained (optional)
2	to 3 ounces crumbled feta cheese

In a small bowl, whisk together the oil, vinegar, mustard, herbs, and black pepper. Set aside.

In a large mixing bowl, combine the rice, tomatoes, scallions, cucumber, garlic, and black olives. Blend in the vinegar, chickpeas, and feta. Chill for 1 hour before serving, allowing the flavors to mingle.

Fluff the salad and serve over a bed of lettuce.

Yield: 6 servings

Rice Advice

During the summer months, try adding fresh parsley, marjoram, or basil.

Black-Eyed Pea, Corn, and Brown Rice Salad

This high-fiber, high-spirited salad shows just how versatile brown rice can be. The subtly sweet black-eyed peas complement the nutty nuance of brown rice.

3	tablespoons canola oil
2	tablespoons red wine vinegar
1	teaspoon Dijon-style mustard
3	to 4 tablespoons chopped fresh parsley (or 2 tablespoons dried)
1/2	teaspoon ground black pepper
1/4	teaspoon salt
1	(15-ounce) can black-eyed peas, drained
2	cups cooked long grain brown rice
1 1/2	cups cooked corn kernels, fresh or frozen
2	cloves garlic, minced
2	large scallions, chopped
2	tablespoons chopped pimentos or roasted sweet peppers

In a large mixing bowl, whisk together the oil, vinegar, mustard, and seasonings. Blend in the black-eyed peas, rice, corn, garlic, scallions, and pimentos. Chill for at least 1 hour before serving, allowing the flavors to mingle.

Fluff the salad and serve over a bed of lettuce.

Yield: 4 servings

Rice Primavera Salad

Primavera refers to spring vegetables, but I also associate it with the optimism that comes with spring. In this picturesque salad, arugula, basil, and spring vegetables give rice a taste of spring.

3	tablespoons olive oil
1¹/₂	tablespoons red wine vinegar or balsamic vinegar
1	teaspoon Dijon-style mustard
2	cloves garlic, minced
10	to 12 large leaves arugula, chopped
¹/₄	cup chopped fresh watercress or basil
2	tablespoons chopped fresh parsley
¹/₂	teaspoon ground black pepper
¹/₄	teaspoon salt
3	to 4 cups cooked long grain white rice or brown rice
2	large tomatoes, diced
1	yellow bell pepper, seeded and diced
1	cup cooked or canned red kidney beans
2	large scallions, chopped
8	to 10 asparagus spears, blanched and coarsely chopped

In a large mixing bowl, whisk together the oil, vinegar, mustard, garlic, herbs, and seasonings. Blend in the rice, tomatoes, bell pepper, beans, scallions, and asparagus. Chill for at least 1 hour before serving.

Serve the salad over a bed of greens.

Yield: 4 to 6 servings

Southwestern Rice Salad with Black Beans and Cilantro

I am quite fond of the big, bold flavors of Southwestern cooking. The quartet of cilantro, cumin, lime, and chiles leaves a pleasurable feeling on the tip of the tongue. This salad captures the breezy spirit of Southwestern food.

3	tablespoons canola oil
	Juice of 1 to 2 limes
1/4	cup chopped fresh cilantro
2	cloves garlic, minced
1	jalapeño pepper, seeded and minced
1	teaspoon ground cumin
1/2	teaspoon ground black pepper
1/2	teaspoon salt
2	medium tomatoes, diced
1	(15-ounce) can black beans, drained
4	cups cooked long grain white rice or brown rice
2	cups cooked corn kernels, fresh or frozen
4	scallions, chopped
1	cup peeled, shredded jicama (optional)
1/4	cup chopped roasted sweet peppers or pimentos

In a large mixing bowl, whisk together the oil, lime juice, cilantro, garlic, jalapeño, and seasonings. Blend in the remaining ingredients and chill for at least 1 hour before serving, allowing the flavors to mingle.

Fluff the salad and serve over a bed of lettuce.

Yield: 6 servings

Rice Advice

For an even spicier salad, try adding one or two roasted New Mexico or poblano chiles along with the jalapeño. Jicama (sometimes called Mexican potato) has a thin brown skin, crisp white flesh, and a flavor similar to a water chestnut. It is best eaten raw.

Wild Rice and Quinoa Salad

*Wild rice, a native grain of North America, meets quinoa,
an ancient grain of South America. Quinoa (pronounced
"keen-wa") is a tiny, ringlike grain with a nutty flavor and
large stockpile of protein. Together this trans-American duo
makes an impressive salad combination.*

$1/2$	cup wild rice
$1 1/2$	cups hot water
1	cup quinoa, rinsed
2	cups water
3	or 4 scallions, chopped
2	cloves garlic, minced
$1/2$	cup diced roasted sweet red pepper
2	to 3 tablespoons canola oil
1	tablespoon red wine vinegar
2	tablespoons chopped fresh parsley
1	teaspoon dried thyme
1	teaspoon Dijon-style mustard
$3/4$	teaspoon ground black pepper
$1/2$	teaspoon salt

Combine the wild rice and hot water in a saucepan and cover. Cook over low-medium heat for 40 to 45 minutes until the rice is tender. Fluff and set aside until the quinoa is done.

Meanwhile, combine the quinoa and water in another saucepan and bring to a boil. Cover and cook for about 15 minutes over low-medium heat, until all of the water is absorbed. Fluff and set aside for 5 minutes.

Combine all of the ingredients in a mixing bowl. Chill for at least 1 hour before serving. Serve over a bed of greens and garnish with sliced tomatoes and cucumbers.

Yield: 4 to 6 servings

Rice Advice

Quinoa is available in most natural food stores and well-stocked grocery stores. Rinse the quinoa thoroughly to wash away a natural, bitter tasting resin that coats the grains.

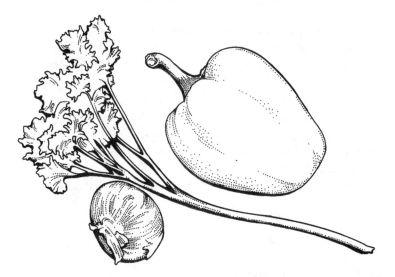

Lemony Artichoke and Rice Salad

Artichokes give this citrusy rice salad a sophisticated air. Fresh herbs lend a fragrant touch.

1/2	pound green beans, cut into 1-inch sections
1	(14-ounce) can artichoke hearts, rinsed and drained
4	cups cooked long grain white rice or brown rice
4	scallions, chopped
2	tomatoes, diced
1	small cucumber, peeled and diced
3	tablespoons olive oil or canola oil
	Juice of 2 lemons
1/4	cup chopped fresh parsley
2	or 3 tablespoons chopped fresh basil
1	teaspoon salt
1/2	teaspoon ground black pepper

Place the green beans in boiling water to cover and cook over high heat for about 3 minutes, until tender. (You may also steam the beans.) Cool the beans in colander under cold running water.

In a large mixing bowl, combine the artichokes, rice, scallions, tomatoes, and cucumber. In a separate bowl, whisk the oil, lemon juice, herbs, and seasonings. Blend into the rice mixture and chill for about 1 hour before serving, allowing the flavors to meld together.

Fluff the salad and serve over a bed of leaf lettuce.

Yield: 4 to 6 servings

Rice Advice

As a general rule, artichokes packed in water have fewer calories than those packed in oil.

Curried Rice, Carrot, and Raisin Salad

For this brightly flavored salad, the curry spices are cooked into the rice and vegetables. A light cilantro dressing coats the grains and perks up the salad without overpowering it.

1	tablespoon canola oil
1	medium onion, chopped
2	large carrots, peeled and sliced
1½	cups long grain white rice or basmati
2	tomatoes, diced
1½	teaspoons curry powder
½	teaspoon salt
¼	teaspoon ground black pepper
¼	teaspoon ground turmeric
2	cups hot water
¾	cup raisins
2	tablespoons olive oil
1	tablespoon red wine vinegar
2	to 3 tablespoons chopped fresh cilantro

Heat the oil in a saucepan and add the onion and carrots. Sauté for 3 to 4 minutes. Stir in rice, tomatoes, and seasonings and cook for 1 minute more over low heat, stirring frequently. Add the water and raisins and bring to a boil. Cover and cook for 15 to 20 minutes over low heat. Remove from the heat and fluff. Let stand for 10 minutes.

While the rice is cooking, make the dressing. In a small bowl, whisk together the olive oil, vinegar, and cilantro. Set aside until the rice is done.

Blend the dressing into the finished rice. Cover and refrigerate for at least 1 hour before serving. Serve the salad over a bed of greens.

Yield: 4 servings

Herb-Scented Lentil and Rice Salad

Lentils are one of the easiest legumes to cook and digest. Unlike beans, lentils do not require soaking in water before cooking and take only about 45 minutes to cook. Lentils add substance and texture to this hearty herbal rice salad.

1/2	cup green lentils, rinsed
3	cups water
3	tablespoons olive oil
	Juice of 1 lemon
1/2	teaspoon Dijon-style mustard
2	cloves garlic, minced
1/4	cup chopped fresh parsley (2 tablespoons dried)
1	teaspoon ground cumin
3/4	teaspoon salt
1/4	teaspoon ground cayenne pepper
4	cups cooked white basmati or long grain rice
2	tomatoes, diced
2	large scallions, chopped
1	green or yellow bell pepper, seeded and diced
1	large carrot, peeled and shredded
1/4	cup chopped fresh basil, arugula, or cilantro

Combine the lentils and water in a saucepan and cook over low heat for about 45 minutes until the lentils are tender. Drain any excess water and let the lentils cool to room temperature.

Meanwhile, in a large mixing bowl, whisk together the oil, lemon juice, mustard, garlic, parsley, and seasonings. Blend in the lentils, rice, tomatoes, scallions, bell pepper, carrot, and herbs. Chill for at least 1 hour before serving, allowing the flavors to mingle.

Serve the salad over a bed of greens.

Yield: 6 servings

Rice Advice

Let the season guide your selection of fresh herbs. Arugula and cilantro are spring and late summer herbs, while basil hails in mid-summer. If none of these are available, there is always parsley.

Thai Black Rice Salad

This striking, eye-catching salad effuses exotic Asian flavors. If you can't find black rice, Lundberg Family Farms' russet Wehani rice or black rice blend make fine substitutes.

1½ cups black rice or Wehani rice
3¼ cups hot water
3   tablespoons light soy sauce
2   tablespoons canola oil or peanut oil
1   tablespoon rice vinegar
1   teaspoon sesame oil
2   tablespoons chopped fresh cilantro
2   cloves garlic, minced
½   teaspoon ground black pepper
1   large tomato, diced
1   green or yellow bell pepper, seeded and chopped
3   or 4 scallions, chopped
1   lime, cut into 6 wedges (optional)

Combine the rice and water in a saucepan and bring to a boil. Cover and cook over low heat for about 40 minutes until the rice is tender. Fluff and let stand for 10 to 15 minutes.

Meanwhile, in a large mixing bowl, whisk together the soy sauce, oil, vinegar, sesame oil, cilantro, garlic, and black pepper. Blend in the tomato, bell pepper, and scallions. Fold in the rice. Chill for at least 1 hour before serving, allowing the flavors to mingle.

Fluff the salad and serve over a bed of lettuce. Garnish with the lime wedges.

Yield: 4 servings

Rice Advice

Black rice is available in well-stocked Asian grocery stores and some specialty gourmet markets. For the kind of presentation that makes the covers of food magazines, serve the salad in the same bowl as a white rice salad (such as Rice Primavera Salad, page 53). Arrange each salad half-moon style.

Grilled Garden Salad

As a grilling enthusiast, I am always on red alert for a new barbecued creation. This dish fills the bill (and the plate) wonderfully. Grilled vegetables infuse a rice salad with a smoky, summery taste of the great outdoors.

2	tablespoons olive oil
	Juice of 1 lemon
2	cloves garlic, minced
2	to 3 tablespoons minced fresh parsley
1	teaspoon ground cumin
1/2	teaspoon ground black pepper
1/2	teaspoon salt
1	small eggplant, halved lengthwise
2	green or red bell peppers
2	plum tomatoes
1	small zucchini, halved lengthwise
1	red onion, peeled and halved
4	cups cooked long grain white rice or brown rice
1	cup cooked or canned red kidney beans
2	or 3 tablespoons chopped fresh basil or arugula (optional)

Preheat the grill until the coals are gray to white.

Combine the olive oil, lemon juice, garlic, parsley, and seasonings in a large mixing bowl. Set aside.

When the fire is ready, place all of the vegetables on the lightly oiled grill. Cook each side for 7 to 10 minutes, until the vegetables are tender and grid-marked. Using tongs, occasionally turn the vegetables as they cook. Remove the grilled vegetables from the fire and place on a cutting board. Let them cool slightly.

Using a butter knife, scrape off any charred parts. Coarsely chop the vegetables and toss together with the dressing. Blend in the rice, beans, and herbs. Chill for 1 hour before serving, allowing the flavors to mingle.

Yield: 4 servings

Rice Advice

For a taste of the Southwest, grill and chop 1 or 2 fresh New Mexico or poblano chiles and toss into the salad. Grilled button mushrooms also make a tasty addition.

Tofu and Rice Salad with Javanese Peanut Dressing

I've discovered the best way to cook with tofu: roast it first. Give it some texture. Roasted tofu acquires a chewy meatiness and blends nicely into rice salads and other dishes. For this lunch salad, tofu teams up with rice, vegetables, water chestnuts, and a dazzling peanut dressing.

1/2	pound extra-firm tofu, cut into 1/2-inch cubes
1/4	cup hot water
3	tablespoons chunky peanut butter
2	tablespoons light soy sauce
1	tablespoon rice vinegar
2	cloves garlic, minced
1	Thai chile or jalapeño pepper, seeded and minced
1	teaspoon sesame oil
2	tablespoons chopped fresh mint
2	tablespoons chopped fresh cilantro
3	cups cooked long grain white rice or brown rice
1	red bell pepper, seeded and diced
3	or 4 scallions, chopped
4	ounces canned water chestnuts, drained

Preheat the oven to 375° F.

Place the tofu on a lightly greased baking pan and roast for 15 to 20 minutes in the oven until lightly browned. Remove from the oven and let cool slightly.

Meanwhile, in a large mixing bowl, whisk together the water, peanut butter, soy sauce, vinegar, garlic, chile, sesame oil, and herbs. Blend in the rice, bell pepper, scallions, water chestnuts, and tofu, coating the grains and vegetables completely with the dressing. Chill for at least 1 hour before serving, allowing the flavors to meld together.

Fluff the salad before serving. Serve over a bed of lettuce and garnish with any remaining herbs.

Yield: 4 to 6 servings

Pesto Rice and Zucchini Salad

When I make a pesto dish, the aroma pervades the kitchen; you can smell it two blocks away. It is exhilarating. This salad celebrates the glory of pesto.

4   cups cooked long grain white rice or brown rice
1   medium zucchini, halved lengthwise and sliced
1   medium carrot, peeled and shredded
1   cup cooked or canned white or red kidney beans
1/2 cup diced roasted sweet red peppers
1 1/2 cups Arugula Basil Pesto (page 174) or Spinach Pesto (page 173), or your favorite pesto sauce

Combine all of the ingredients in a large mixing bowl. Chill for 1 hour to allow the flavors to mingle.

Serve over a bed of lettuce and garnish with chopped ripe tomatoes and cucumber.

Yield: 6 servings

Confetti Riz Cous and White Bean Salad

For this salad, riz cous (a brown rice product similar to couscous) blends with a variety of summer vegetables.

1	cup riz cous
2	cups hot water
2	plum tomatoes, diced
1	small cucumber, diced
2	large scallions, chopped
2	cloves garlic, minced
1	cup cooked or canned small white beans, drained
1	cup fresh green peas, blanched
2 1/2	tablespoons olive oil
1 1/2	tablespoons balsamic vinegar
1/2	teaspoon salt
1/2	teaspoon ground black pepper
1/4	cup chopped mixture of fresh garden herbs (such as basil, parsley, mint, and oregano)

Combine the riz cous and water in a saucepan and bring to a boil. Cover and cook for 4 to 5 minutes over low heat, until all of the liquid is absorbed. Fluff the grains and let stand for about 5 minutes more.

In a mixing bowl, combine the riz cous with the remaining ingredients and toss together. Chill for 1 hour before serving.

Yield: 4 to 6 servings

Emily's Pepperoncini Rice Salad

My resourceful friend Emily Robin has a talent for fashioning fabulous salads. Her culinary muse is inspired by whatever's in the kitchen. Here she combines leftover rice and vegetables, sundry pantry staples, and chickpeas; the results are astoundingly good.

4	tablespoons olive oil
2	tablespoons rice vinegar or apple cider vinegar
1	teaspoon Dijon-style mustard
2	tablespoons chopped fresh parsley (or 1 tablespoon dried)
1	teaspoon dried basil
1/2	teaspoon ground black pepper
1/4	teaspoon garlic powder
1/4	teaspoon salt
3	cups cooked long grain white rice, basmati or Texmati
3	or 4 pepperoncini, seeded and chopped
2	plum tomatoes, diced
2	medium carrots, peeled and sliced
1	cup cooked or canned chickpeas, drained
1/4	to 1/2 cup shredded lowfat Swiss cheese or part-skim mozzarella

In a large mixing bowl, whisk together the oil, vinegar, mustard, and seasonings. Blend in the remaining ingredients and chill for 1 hour before serving, allowing the flavors to meld together.

Serve the salad over a large pile of leaf greens or chopped spinach.

Yield: 4 servings

Rice Advice

Pepperoncinis are pickled Italian peppers usually found in the Italian section of grocery stores. They are not in any way related to pepperoni.

Miami Rice and Avocado Salad

On a recent trip to South Florida I discovered that Miami has become a culinary melting pot of Caribbean, Latin American, and native Floridian tastes. This artful salad was inspired by one of my many memorable meals on South Beach.

3	tablespoons canola oil
	Juice of 1 to 2 limes
2	tablespoons chopped fresh cilantro
2	cloves garlic, minced
1	jalapeño pepper, seeded and minced (optional)
1	teaspoon ground cumin
1/2	teaspoon ground black pepper
3/4	teaspoon salt
3	cups cooked long grain white rice or brown rice
2	or 3 ripe avocados, peeled, pitted, and diced
1	red or yellow bell pepper, seeded, and diced
1	large tomato, diced
1	cup canned or cooked black beans
4	scallions, chopped

In a large mixing bowl, whisk together the oil, lime juice, cilantro, garlic, jalapeño, and seasonings. Blend in the remaining ingredients. Chill the salad for at least 1 hour before serving, allowing the flavors to mingle.

When you are ready to serve, fluff the salad and serve over a bed of lettuce. Garnish with slices of mango or star fruit.

Yield: 6 servings

Rice Advice

You can judge the ripeness of an avocado by holding it in the palm of your hand and pressing down gently with your thumb; a ripe avocado should give slightly.

Beet and Rice Salad with Balsamic Dill Vinaigrette

Roasting is the way to cook beets; the true essence is liberated. Roasted beets turn this rice salad a lively purplish pink. The rice and beet combination is nicely balanced by fresh dill and red onion.

4	medium beets, scrubbed and rinsed
3	tablespoons canola oil or olive oil
2	tablespoons balsamic vinegar
1	teaspoon Dijon-style mustard
3	tablespoons chopped fresh dill
1/2	teaspoon ground black pepper
1/2	teaspoon salt
3	cups cooked long grain white rice or brown rice
2	stalks celery, finely chopped
1	small red onion, thinly sliced

Preheat the oven to 375° F.

Wrap the beets in aluminum foil and place in a baking pan. Roast for 50 minutes to 1 hour, until the beets are tender. Remove the beets from the oven, unwrap, and let cool.

Meanwhile, in a mixing bowl, whisk together the oil, vinegar, mustard, dill, and seasonings. When the beets are cool enough to handle, peel off any blemishes or loose skin. Coarsely chop the beets and add to the vinaigrette; coat thoroughly. Blend in the rice, celery, and onion. Refrigerate for 1 hour to allow the flavors to mingle.

Serve the salad over a bed of leaf lettuce and garnish with any extra sprigs of dill.

Yield: 4 to 6 servings

Chapter 3
Side Dishes with Panache

This chapter is the story of the reawakening of rice in the American kitchen. For generations a side dish of rice meant a pile of plain, meekly flavored granules topped with butter. The side dish rarely attracted any attention nor woke up anyone's taste buds. Ethnic dishes were interesting but often overlooked.

Rice was dull.

Luckily, those flavor-deficient days are over. This chapter features a tantalizing array of international dishes with assertive flavors, from Chipotle Rice and Beans, Festive Yellow Rice, and *Risi e Bisi* to Curried Rice and Peas, and Pumpkin Pilau. Leafy greens, winter squash, spinach, plantains, curry, and chiles all make frequent appearances. There are also multitudinous variations on rice and beans, the quintessential side dish, the granddaddy of them all. Rice on the side will never be the same.

Even if one is pressed for time, it's still easy to assemble a nourishing side of rice with very little effort. The fastest way is to add a vegetable to the pot of rice while it cooks. There are several rice-friendly vegetables that cook up nicely in the same pot, such as diced sweet potatoes, carrots, sweet peas, butternut squash, spinach, and asparagus. By adding these ingredients, you will increase both the nutritional value and the flavor of a meal and help defeat the forces of mediocrity.

Greens, Rice, and Beans

Rice goes well with hardy greens. A plethora of leafy vegetables is available throughout the year, including escarole, kale, dandelion greens, curly endive, and Russian kale. You can extend their domain well beyond garnishes and tossed salads: these crunchy greens add valuable nutrients, flavors, and textures to rice dishes.

1	tablespoon canola oil
1	medium yellow onion, diced
2	cloves garlic, minced
3	cups hot water
1 1/2	cups long grain white rice or parboiled rice
2	cups packed, chopped dandelion greens, curly endive, or kale
1/4	cup chopped fresh parsley (or 2 tablespoons dried)
1/2	teaspoon salt
1/2	teaspoon ground black pepper
1	(15-ounce) can red kidney beans or other kind of beans, drained and heated

Heat the oil in a saucepan and add the onion and garlic. Sauté for about 5 minutes. Add the water, rice, greens, and seasonings and bring to a boil. Cover and cook for 15 to 20 minutes over low heat. Stir in the beans and turn off the heat. Let stand for 5 to 10 minutes before serving.

Yield: 4 servings

Chipotle Rice and Beans

Chipotle peppers have a way of waking up an otherwise quiet and sedate meal. They impart a smoky, peppery heat to this rice and beans dish and turn the mild to wild.

1	tablespoon canola oil
1	small red onion, diced
2	cloves garlic, minced
1	or 2 canned chipotle peppers, minced
3	cups hot water
1 1/2	cups long grain white rice or parboiled rice
2	tablespoons dried parsley
1/2	teaspoon salt
1	(15-ounce) can black beans, red kidney beans, or other kind of beans, drained and heated

Heat the oil in a saucepan and add the onion, garlic, and chipotle pepper. Sauté for about 5 minutes. Add the water, rice, and seasonings and bring to a boil. Cover and cook for 15 to 20 minutes over low heat.

Stir in the beans and turn off the heat. Let stand for 5 to 10 minutes before serving.

Yield: 4 servings

Pumpkin Pilau

In the Caribbean I learned about cooking pumpkin with rice. The West Indian pumpkin (also called calabaza) has a brilliantly orange, dense flesh and sweet potato–like flavor that meshes well with rice and curry.

1	tablespoon canola oil
1	medium yellow onion, chopped
2	cloves garlic, minced
2	teaspoons minced fresh ginger root
2	cups peeled, diced West Indian pumpkin or other winter squash
2 1/2	teaspoons curry powder
1/2	teaspoon ground black pepper
1/2	teaspoon salt
1/4	teaspoon ground cumin
1/4	teaspoon ground turmeric
3	cups hot water
1 1/2	cups long grain white rice or parboiled rice
1 1/2	cups coarsely chopped kale or spinach

Heat the oil in a saucepan and add the onion, garlic, and ginger. Sauté for 5 to 7 minutes. Stir in the pumpkin and seasonings and cook for 1 minute more over low heat.

Stir in the water and rice and bring to a boil. Cover and cook for about 15 minutes over low heat. Stir in the kale and cook for 5 to 10 minutes more. Fluff the rice and turn off the heat. Let stand for 10 minutes before serving.

Yield: 4 to 6 servings

Rice Advice

West Indian pumpkin is sold in large watermelon-like wedges in Caribbean and Latin American markets and well stocked supermarkets. You can substitute hubbard squash, butternut squash, or sugar pie pumpkin.

Fire and Rice

Connoisseurs of spicy food will appreciate this devilishly hot dish. A trio of peppers—jalapeño, chipotle, and cayenne— dance a zippity-do-da on the tip of the tongue and leave smoldering embers of flavor in their wake.

1	tablespoon canola oil
1	medium yellow onion, diced
2	cloves garlic, minced
1	or 2 large jalapeño or Red Fresno peppers, seeded and minced
1	large tomato, diced
1	large chipotle pepper, seeded and minced
2	tablespoons fresh parsley (or 1 tablespoon dried)
1	teaspoon paprika
1/2	teaspoon salt
1/4	teaspoon ground cayenne pepper
2 1/2	cups hot water
1 1/4	cups long grain white rice, basmati or parboiled rice

Heat the oil in a saucepan and add the onion, garlic, and jalapeno. Sauté for about 4 minutes. Stir in the tomato, chipotle, and seasonings and sauté for 2 minutes more. Add the water and rice and bring to a boil. Cover and cook over low heat for 15 to 20 minutes until the rice is tender. Remove from the heat and let stand for 5 to 10 minutes.

Fluff the rice and serve hot.

Yield: 4 servings

Rice Advice

If you are extremely fond of fiery fare, puncture a whole Scotch bonnet pepper with a fork and let it simmer with the rice and water. Remove it when the rice has finished cooking; cut into strips and serve on the side.

Orzo Pilaf

Here's a quick and simple dish with enticing flavors and golden hues. Orzo is a small, rice-shaped pasta that pairs up well with rice. It is a favorite staple in Middle Eastern pilafs.

1	tablespoon olive oil
1	medium yellow onion, chopped
2	tablespoons minced shallots
1	cup long grain white rice or parboiled rice
1/2	cup orzo
1/2	teaspoon salt
1/4	teaspoon ground black pepper
1/4	teaspoon ground turmeric
2 1/2	cups hot water
1	cup cooked chickpeas, drained and heated (optional)

Heat the oil in a medium saucepan and add the onion and shallots. Sauté for 3 to 4 minutes. Stir in the rice, orzo, and seasonings and cook for 1 minute more over low heat, stirring frequently. Add the water and bring to a boil. Cover and cook for 15 to 20 minutes over low heat.

Remove from the heat and fluff the rice. If you'd like, stir in the chickpeas. Let stand for 10 minutes before serving.

Yield: 4 servings

Rice Advice

Orzo is also called rosa marina. Look for it in the Italian section of the grocery store.

Curried Rice and Peas

Although there are copious recipes for rice and peas, each has its own distinct personality and flavor niche; I never tire of them. This Indian rendition is spiced with a trace of ginger and curry.

1	tablespoon canola oil
1	small red onion, chopped
2	teaspoons minced fresh ginger
1	large tomato, diced
1	teaspoon ground cumin
1/2	teaspoon ground turmeric
1/2	teaspoon salt
1/8	to 1/4 teaspoon ground cayenne
1 1/2	cups white basmati rice
1	cup green peas, fresh or frozen
3	cups hot water
2	scallions, chopped

Heat the oil in a saucepan and add the onion and ginger. Sauté for 3 to 4 minutes. Add the tomato and seasonings and cook for 1 minute more over low heat. Stir in the rice, peas, and water and bring to a boil. Cover and cook for 15 to 20 minutes over low heat, until the rice is tender.

Remove from the heat, fluff the rice, and stir in the scallions. Let stand for 5 to 10 minutes before serving.

Yield: 4 servings

Jamaican Cook-up Rice

"Cook up rice" is a one-pot meal consisting of whatever vegetables happen to be in the kitchen. The coconut flavored broth adds a nutty tropical nuance. You can serve it as either a side dish or a main dish.

1	tablespoon canola oil
1	medium yellow or red onion, diced
1	green bell pepper, seeded and diced
1	small zucchini, diced
8	to 10 mushrooms, sliced
1/2	Scotch bonnet pepper, seeded and minced (optional)
2	cups hot water
1	cup light coconut milk or rice milk
1 1/2	cups long grain white rice
2	cups peeled, diced winter squash, sweet potato, or carrots
2	tablespoons dried parsley
1	teaspoon dried thyme
1/2	teaspoon ground allspice
1/2	teaspoon salt
2	cups chopped leafy greens (kale, chard, beet greens, or spinach)

Heat the oil in a saucepan and add the onion, bell pepper, zucchini, mushrooms, and Scotch bonnet pepper. Sauté for 5 to 7 minutes. Add the water, coconut milk, rice, winter squash, and seasonings and bring to a boil. Cover and cook for 15 to 20 minutes over low heat.

Fluff the rice and stir in the greens. Let stand for about 10 minutes before serving.

Yield: 4 to 6 servings

Rice Advice

The Scotch bonnet pepper is a curvy, colorful chile native to Jamaica and qualifies as the world's hottest pod. It is available fresh in specialty produce aisles of large supermarkets and Latin American markets. For a milder version, try a jalapeño chile.

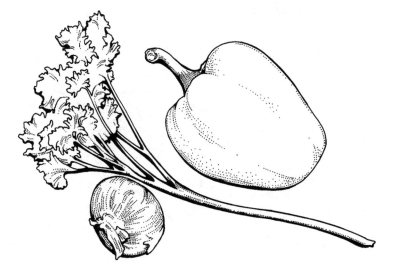

South Indian Eggplant Rice

For this flavorful dish, basmati rice is cooked separately and then combined with eggplant and spices (like mixing a rice salad). A fresh tomato replaces some of the oil that would normally be used.

1 1/2	cups white basmati rice
3	cups hot water
1 1/2	tablespoons canola oil
1	small yellow onion, chopped
1	medium eggplant, diced
1	large tomato, diced
1	small hot chile pepper, seeded and minced
1	teaspoon ground cumin
1/2	teaspoon garam masala
1/2	teaspoon mustard seeds
1/2	teaspoon salt
1/4	teaspoon ground turmeric
	Juice of 1 large lemon

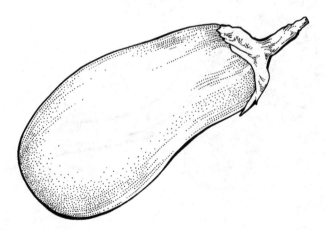

Place the rice and water in saucepan and bring to a boil. Cover and cook for 15 to 20 minutes over low heat, until the rice is tender. Set aside for 5 to 10 minutes.

Meanwhile, heat the oil in another saucepan and add the onion, eggplant, and tomato. Cook for 8 to 10 minutes over medium heat, stirring frequently, until the eggplant is tender. Blend in the chile pepper and seasonings and cook for 1 minute more. Remove from the heat.

When the rice is done, fold it into the vegetable mixture. Blend in the lemon juice. Serve the side dish with lowfat plain yogurt on the side.

Yield: 6 servings

Rice Advice

Garam masala is a fragrant spice blend available in Indian markets, natural food stores, and well-stocked supermarkets. If you do not have it, try adding 1/4 teaspoon each of ground cumin and coriander and a scant touch of ground cloves.

Greek Spinach Pilaf

Called spanakorizo, *this side dish is a tasty union of spinach and rice. A triumvirate of Greek herbs—mint, oregano, and thyme—contribute an undertone of earthy herbal flavors.*

1	tablespoon olive oil
1	medium yellow onion, chopped
2	tablespoons tomato paste
1	(10-ounce) bag fresh spinach, rinsed, trimmed, and coarsely chopped
1	cup long grain white rice or parboiled rice
2	cups hot water
2	tablespoons chopped fresh mint (or 2 teaspoons dried)
1 1/2	teaspoons dried oregano
1	teaspoon dried thyme
1/2	teaspoon ground black pepper
1/2	teaspoon salt
2	to 3 ounces crumbled feta cheese (optional)

Heat the oil in a large saucepan and add the onion. Sauté for 4 minutes. Reduce the heat to low and blend in the tomato paste. Stir in the spinach and cook for 2 to 3 minutes more until wilted. Stir in the rice, water, and seasonings and bring to a boil. Cover and cook for 15 to 20 minutes over low heat until the rice is tender.

Fluff the rice and turn off the heat. Let stand for 5 to 10 minutes before serving. If you'd like, sprinkle the feta over the rice before serving.

Yield: 4 servings

Nutty Whole Grain Pilaf

There is something intrinsically comforting about the sight of whole grain pilaf. It simply must be good for you. Long grain brown rice is a natural for this dish, but I also like fancy rices such as russet-colored Wehani, black rice, or whole grain blends.

1	tablespoon olive oil
1	medium yellow onion, diced
1	green or red bell pepper, seeded and diced
2	tablespoons minced shallots, or 2 cloves garlic, minced
1	cup Wehani rice, long grain brown rice, or a black rice blend
2¹/₄	cups hot water
2	tablespoons minced fresh parsley (about 1 table-spoon dried)
¹/₂	teaspoon ground black pepper
¹/₂	teaspoon salt
¹/₂	cup roasted unsalted cashews or slivered almonds

Heat the oil in a saucepan and add the onion, bell pepper, and shallots. Sauté for about 4 minutes. Stir in the rice, water, and seasonings and bring to a boil. Cover and cook for about 40 minutes over low heat until the rice is tender.

Fluff the rice and stir in the nuts. Let stand for 5 to 10 minutes before serving.

Yield: 4 servings

Middle Eastern Rice with Lentils

You can trace the pedigree of this dish back for centuries. Called mujadarrah, this wholesome stew has a stick-to-your-ribs quality to it. My grandmother makes it with white rice; brown rice is a third generation improvisation.

3/4 cup green lentils, rinsed
41/4 cups water
1/2 cup long grain brown rice or brown basmati
3/4 teaspoon salt
1/2 teaspoon ground coriander or cumin
1/2 teaspoon ground black pepper
1 tablespoon olive oil
1 medium yellow onion, thinly sliced

Combine the lentils and water in a saucepan and cook for about 20 minutes over low-medium heat. Stir in the rice and cook for 30 to 40 minutes more over low heat, until the lentils and rice are tender. Stir in the seasonings and remove from the heat. Let stand for 5 to 10 minutes before serving.

Meanwhile, in another skillet, heat the oil and add the onion. Sauté for 7 to 10 minutes, until golden brown and wilted. Stir the onions into the pot of cooked lentils and rice (or serve over the top). Serve with warm pita bread.

Yield: 4 servings

Rice Advice

If you prefer to use white rice, add the rice after the lentils have cooked for 35 minutes (and cook for 25 to 30 minutes more).

Spinach Basmati Rice

This is an easy dish for the time-challenged cook (i.e. harried). Garam masala and cardamom add a delicate perfume-like essence and spinach delivers valuable nutrients and flavor.

1	tablespoon canola oil
1	medium yellow onion, diced
2	cloves garlic, minced
1/2	teaspoon garam masala
1/2	teaspoon salt
1/4	teaspoon ground cardamom
1 1/2	cups white basmati or long grain white rice
3	cups hot water
1	(10-ounce) package frozen chopped spinach, thawed and drained

Heat the oil in a saucepan and add the onion and garlic. Cook over medium heat for 4 minutes, stirring frequently. Stir in the seasonings and rice and cook for 1 minute more over low heat. Stir in the water and spinach and bring to a boil. Cover and cook for 15 to 20 minutes over low heat.

Turn off the heat and fluff the rice while stirring the spinach. Let stand for 5 to 10 minutes before serving.

Yield: 6 servings

Rice Advice

Garam masala is available in Indian markets, natural food stores, and well-stocked supermarkets. If you do not have it, try adding 1/4 teaspoon each of ground cumin and coriander and a scant touch of ground cloves.

Festive Yellow Rice

This brightly hued dish is scented with ginger, lemongrass, and a hint of turmeric. It is called nasi kuning in Indonesia, where it is served at festive celebrations. For an authentic presentation, mound the rice in the center of a large plate and arrange a variety of dishes around the edge.

1	tablespoon canola oil
2	tablespoons minced shallots or red onion
2	teaspoons minced fresh ginger root
2	teaspoons minced fresh lemongrass
1	teaspoon ground coriander
1/2	teaspoon ground turmeric
1/2	teaspoon salt
1/4	teaspoon ground cayenne pepper
1/3	cup currants or raisins
1	cup long grain white, basmati, or jasmine rice
2	cups hot water

Heat the oil in a saucepan and add the shallots, ginger, and lemongrass. Sauté for 2 to 3 minutes. Add the seasonings and cook for 1 minute more. Stir in the currants, rice, and water and bring to a boil. Cover and cook for 15 to 20 minutes over low heat, until the rice is tender.

Remove from the heat and fluff the rice. Let stand for 5 to 10 minutes before serving.

Yield: 4 servings

Rice Advice

Lemongrass is a brittle, lemon-scented herb available in Asian markets and the specialty produce sections of large grocery stores.

Jasmine Rice with Mixed Leafy Greens

Jasmine's popcornlike aroma matches up well with strongly flavored seasonal leafy greens. I make this dish with the best-looking greens I can find at the grocery store (or in my garden).

3	cups hot water
1 1/2	cups jasmine rice
2	carrots, peeled and diced
1	large tomato, chopped
2	tablespoons chopped fresh parsley (1 tablespoon dried)
1/2	teaspoon ground black pepper
1/2	teaspoon salt
2	to 3 cups mixture of chopped kale, mustard greens, dandelion greens, or curly endive

In a medium saucepan, combine the water, rice, carrots, tomato, seasonings, and greens and bring to a boil. Cover and cook for 15 to 20 minutes over low heat.

Fluff the rice and let stand for 5 to 10 minutes before serving.

Yield: 4 servings

Rice Advice

Add 1 (15-ounce) can of black beans, red kidney beans, or black-eyed peas to the rice. In the spring I'll add 6 to 8 chopped asparagus spears along with the carrots.

Risi e Bisi

This creamy Italian version of rice and peas elevates the humble green pea to gourmet status (risi e bisi means rice and peas). It is a baby risotto, of sorts, since it is prepared in a similar fashion.

1	tablespoon olive oil
1	small yellow onion, chopped
1	stalk celery, chopped
1	cup arborio rice or other short grain white rice
3	cups hot water
2	tablespoons chopped fresh parsley (or 1 table-spoon dried)
1/2	teaspoon salt
1/2	teaspoon ground black pepper
1 1/2	cups green peas, fresh or frozen
2	to 3 tablespoons grated Parmesan cheese (optional)

Heat the oil in a saucepan and add the onion and celery. Cook over medium heat for 5 to 7 minutes, stirring frequently. Stir in the rice, 2 cups water, and seasonings and cook over low heat for about 12 minutes, stirring frequently. Gradually stir in the peas and remaining 1 cup water and cook for 7 to 10 minutes more until the rice is tender.

Remove from the heat and stir in the cheese. Let stand for a few minutes before serving. Garnish with any extra sprigs of fresh parsley.

Yield: 4 servings

Hoppin' John

Hoppin' John is a Southern dish of black-eyed peas and rice. This version, sans meat, is rejuvenated with spinach and golden onions. Serving Hoppin' John on New Year's Day is said to bring good luck for the coming year.

2	cups hot water
1	cup long grain white rice or brown rice
1/2	teaspoon salt
1/2	teaspoon ground black pepper
3	cups chopped fresh spinach
1	(15-ounce) can black-eyed peas, drained
1	tablespoon olive oil or canola oil
1	medium yellow onion, slivered

Combine the water, rice, and seasonings in a saucepan and bring to a boil. Stir in the spinach and cover. Cook over low heat for 15 to 20 minutes (about 40 minutes for brown rice). Stir in black-eyed peas and remove from the heat. Let stand for about 10 minutes.

Meanwhile, heat the oil in a skillet and add the onions. Sauté for 5 to 7 minutes, until wilted and golden brown. When the rice has finished cooking, stir the onions into the pot. Serve hot.

Yield: 4 servings

Island Black Beans and Rice

During my heady restaurant days, late-night meals often consisted of a simple (but spicy) combination of black beans and jasmine rice. It always hit the spot after an exhausting day in the kitchen.

1 1/2 cups jasmine rice or white basmati
3   cups hot water
1   tablespoon canola oil
1   medium red onion, diced
1   green pepper, seeded and diced
2   cloves garlic, minced
1   (15-ounce) can black beans, drained
1   (15-ounce) can stewed tomatoes
1/2   teaspoon ground cumin
1/2   teaspoon ground black pepper
1/2   teaspoon salt
1   to 3 teaspoons (depending on your mood) of your favorite Scotch bonnet sauce or other hot pepper sauce

Combine the rice and water in a saucepan and bring to a boil. Cover and cook over low heat for 15 to 20 minutes, until the rice is tender. Remove from the heat and let stand for 10 minutes.

Meanwhile, heat the oil in another saucepan and add the onion, bell pepper, and garlic. Sauté for 5 to 7 minutes. Add the beans, tomatoes, and seasonings and cook for 7 to 10 minutes more over low heat, stirring frequently. When ready to eat, place the rice on serving plates and spoon the stewed beans over the top. Drizzle the hot sauce over the beans.

Yield: 4 servings

Rice Advice

Add 2 tablespoons of chopped fresh cilantro, chives, or parsley to either the rice or beans near the end of the cooking time.

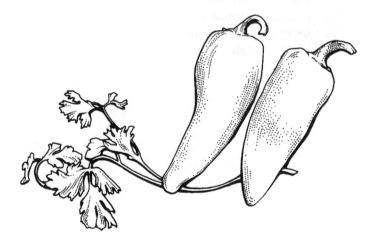

Wild Rice and Plantain Pilaf

Plantains and rice often share the same plate in the Caribbean. Although plantains are traditionally cooked separately and served alongside of rice, occasionally the two are cooked together in the same pot. This pilaf combines the nutty, grassy flavor of wild rice with the bananalike nature of sweet plantains.

1/2	cup wild rice
1 1/2	cups water
1 1/2	tablespoons canola oil
2	sweet yellow plantains, peeled and sliced
1	medium yellow onion, diced
1	green or red bell pepper, seeded and diced
1	jalapeno or Red Fresno pepper, seeded and minced (optional)
1	cup long grain white rice or parboiled rice
2	cups hot water
1	teaspoon paprika
1/2	teaspoon ground black pepper
1/2	teaspoon ground allspice
1/2	teaspoon salt

Combine the wild rice and water in a saucepan and bring to a boil. Cover and cook over low heat for 40 to 45 minutes. Remove from the heat and set aside.

Meanwhile, heat the oil in a saucepan and add the plantains, onion, bell pepper, and jalapeño. Cook for 5 to 7 minutes over medium heat, stirring occasionally. Stir in the rice, hot water, and seasonings and bring to a boil. Cover and cook over low heat for 15 to 20 minutes, until the rice is tender.

Fluff the pilaf and stir in the cooked wild rice. Remove from the heat and let stand for about 10 minutes before serving.

Yield: 4 to 6 servings

Rice Advice

To peel a plantain, remove the tips and cut a lengthwise incision in the skin. Using your thumb, peel the skin back and discard. The plantain is now ready to be sliced.

New Mexico Red Chile Rice

It has become a family ritual: Every August my sister (who lives in Colorado) purchases a crateload of fresh New Mexico chiles at the farmers' market and sends them to me via express mail. For days afterward I prepare a fiesta of dishes infused with roasted New Mexico chiles. Their searing (but not overpowering) heat and signature cherry-like flavor make them a favorite among chile pepper connoisseurs.

1 tablespoon canola oil
1 medium yellow onion, diced
2 cloves garlic, minced
2 to 4 roasted New Mexico red chiles, peeled, seeded, and chopped
3 cups hot water
1 1/2 cups long grain white rice
2 tablespoons fresh parsley (or 1 tablespoon dried)
1 teaspoon ground cumin
1 teaspoon paprika
1/2 teaspoon salt
2 tablespoons minced fresh cilantro (optional)

Heat the oil in a saucepan and add the onion and garlic. Sauté for 3 or 4 minutes. Add the chiles, water, rice, parsley, and dried seasonings and bring to a boil. Cover and cook over low heat for 15 to 20 minutes. Fluff the rice and fold in the cilantro. Let stand for 5 to 10 minutes before serving.

Yield: 4 to 6 servings

Rice Advice

To roast a chile, place the whole pepper over hot coals or fire (or beneath a broiler) and cook until the skin is uniformly charred. Let the chile cool slightly and scrape off the outer burnt skin with a butter knife. Remove the seeds and discard; chop the remaining flesh. Do not place roasted chiles under cold running water—sacrilege! This will cause valuable flavors to be lost. New Mexico chiles are available on a seasonal basis from well-stocked supermarkets.

Creole Red Beans and Rice

If it's Monday in Louisiana country, you'll find red beans and rice on the stove. Traditional recipes call for slowly cooking red beans from scratch, but for this spur-of-the-moment version I use canned beans. I've also left out the ham hocks, etc.

1¼ cups long grain white rice or Wild Pecan rice
2½ cups hot water
1   tablespoon canola oil
1   medium onion, diced
1   green or red bell pepper, seeded and diced
1   stalk celery, chopped
2   cloves garlic, minced
1   (15-ounce) can red kidney beans, drained
1   (14-ounce) can stewed tomatoes
1½ teaspoons dried oregano
½   teaspoon ground black pepper
½   teaspoon salt
¼   teaspoon ground cayenne pepper (optional)
2   tablespoons chopped fresh parsley
     Tabasco, to taste

Combine the rice and water in a saucepan and bring to a boil. Cover and cook for 15 to 20 minutes over low heat. Remove from the heat and fluff the rice. Let stand for 5 to 10 minutes.

Meanwhile, heat the oil in another saucepan and add the onion, bell pepper, celery, and garlic. Sauté for 5 to 7 minutes. Add the beans, tomatoes, and dried seasonings and cook for 10 to 12 minutes over low heat, stirring frequently. Stir in the parsley and remove from the heat.

Spoon the rice onto plates and serve the beans over the top. Pass the Tabasco at the table.

Yield: 3 or 4 servings

Rice Advice
Wild Pecan rice is a native Louisianian rice with a popcorny, pecanlike aroma. Despite its name, it is not blended with either pecans or wild rice.

Drunken Baked Beans and Rice

This version of baked beans and rice smolders with a sweet, barbecued flavor. Almost any bean will suffice, but white beans have an affinity for sweet flavors.

1 cup dried navy beans or great northern beans, soaked and drained
1 tablespoon canola oil
1 medium red onion, diced
2 cloves garlic, minced
1 1/2 cups hot water
1 cup stale beer
1/2 cup ketchup
1/3 cup brown sugar
1/3 cup molasses
3 tablespoons Worcestershire sauce
1/2 teaspoon ground allspice
1/2 teaspoon ground black pepper
1/2 teaspoon salt
1 cup long or short grain white rice or brown rice

Place the beans in plenty of water to cover in a saucepan and cook over low-medium heat for about 1 to 1 1/2 hours until tender. Drain the beans and discard the liquid.

Preheat the oven to 350°F.

In a flameproof casserole dish or Dutch oven, heat the oil and add the onion and garlic. Sauté for about 4 minutes. Stir in the beans, water, beer, ketchup, brown sugar, molasses, Worcestershire sauce, and seasonings and bring to a simmer. Cook for 3 to 4 minutes more over medium heat, stirring occasionally. Stir in the rice and blend well. Cover the casserole and transfer to the oven. Bake for 25 to 30 minutes (40 to 45 minutes for brown rice) until the rice is tender.

Remove from the oven and let stand for 10 minutes before serving. Serve with dark bread.

Yield: 4 to 6 servings

Rice Advice

For tender, plump beans, soak the beans for at least 4 hours, preferably overnight. Discard the soaking liquid and cook the beans in fresh water.

Wild Rice and Basmati Pilaf

This attractive pilaf fills the kitchen with the grassy aroma of wild rice, the popcorn scent of basmati, and the familiar presence of onions and garlic. It whets the appetite and is a sensory delight for the eyes, the nose, and the mouth.

1/2   cup wild rice
1 1/2 cups water
1   tablespoon canola oil
1   medium yellow onion, diced
1   green or red bell pepper, seeded and diced
2   cloves garlic, minced
1   jalapeño pepper, seeded and minced (optional)
1   cup white basmati rice or jasmine rice
2   cups hot water
2   tablespoons chopped fresh parsley (1 tablespoon dried)
1/2   teaspoon dried thyme
1/2   teaspoon ground black pepper
1/2   teaspoon salt

Combine the wild rice and water in a saucepan and bring to a boil. Cover and cook over low heat for 40 to 45 minutes. Remove from the heat and set aside.

Meanwhile, heat the oil in a saucepan and add the onion, bell pepper, garlic, and jalapeño. Cook for 5 to 7 minutes over medium heat, stirring occasionally. Stir in the basmati rice, hot water, and seasonings and bring to a boil. Cover and cook over low heat for 15 to 20 minutes, until the rice is tender. Fluff the pilaf and stir in the wild rice. Remove from the heat and let stand for about 10 minutes before serving.

Yield: 4 servings

Arroz Verde

This staple of Southwestern and Mexican cuisines has a spicy, herbal presence. (Arroz verde means "green rice.") The authentic version calls for poblano chiles, which are emerald green pods with a raisinlike flavor and mellow (but quietly assertive) heat. The chiles are roasted before being added to the rice (see Rice Advice, page 99).

1	tablespoon canola oil
1	medium yellow onion, diced
2	cloves garlic, minced
2	medium roasted poblano chiles, peeled, seeded, and diced
2¹/₂	cups hot water
1¹/₄	cups long grain white rice or brown rice
2	tablespoons fresh parsley (or 1 tablespoon dried)
1	teaspoon ground cumin
¹/₂	teaspoon salt
¹/₄	teaspoon ground black pepper
2	cups chopped, packed fresh spinach
2	tablespoons minced fresh cilantro

In a saucepan, heat the oil and add the onion, garlic, and peppers. Sauté for 5 minutes. Add the water, rice, parsley, dried seasonings, and spinach and bring to a boil. Cover and cook over low heat for 15 to 20 minutes (for brown rice, about 40 minutes). Fluff the rice and stir in the cilantro. Let stand for 5 to 10 minutes before serving.

Yield: 4 servings

Rice Advice

Roasting the chiles removes the tough outer skin and produces a deep, smoky flavor. If poblano chiles are not available (or if you prefer a milder version), substitute 2 green bell peppers. The dish will lack the distinctive flavor of poblano chiles but will still be rewarding.

Chapter 4

Rice around the World

Magnificent Main Entrées

This chapter offers an adventurous taste of the world's vegetarian rice cuisine. The recipes visit every corner of the earth, from South American Vegetable and Rice Stew to West African Jollof Rice, from Country Garden Paella to West Indian Pilau. Discover a host of fascinating dishes such as Vegetable Biryani, Yellow Rice and Black Beans, Jessica's Black Rice and Pumpkin Stew, and other globally inspired dishes.

There is also an impressive tableau of classic and inventive recipes for risotto, the Italian rice dish with a creamy, luscious texture. Unlike most rice dishes, risotto requires frequent stirring and the liquid is added in stages. Risotto owes its distinct nature to arborio rice, a gourmet grain that has recently become widely available. Some of the intriguing versions include Champagne, Mushroom, and Spinach Risotto, Festive Squash and Sweet Pea Risotto, and Beet Root Risotto. Risotto also depends on quality Parmesan or Romano cheese, the kinds found in the cheese section of the grocery store, not the dry goods section.

In addition to exuding an international flair, these vibrant rice suppers include a variety of nutrient-rich vegetables; you'll find dishes with winter squash, potatoes, eggplant, broccoli, peas, and whatever else the green grocer has to offer. Leafy greens such as escarole, kale, and spinach—all rich in vitamins and cancer-fighting antioxidants—make frequent appearances, as well as fiber-rich beans and lentils.

One thing is for certain: When these rice entrées take center stage, the absent fat, salt, cholesterol, and meat surely won't be missed.

South American Vegetable and Rice Stew

This hearty rice stew is adapted from a savory South American dish called locro. It has a wholesome, comforting presence and can be served on a plate or in a bowl.

1	tablespoon canola oil
1	medium yellow onion, diced
2	or 3 cloves garlic, minced
1	jalapeño or Red Fresno pepper, seeded and minced (optional)
1	(14-ounce) can stewed tomatoes
2	tablespoons dried parsley
1	tablespoon paprika
1	tablespoon dried oregano
1/2	teaspoon salt
2	cups peeled, diced butternut or buttercup squash
3	cups hot water
2	cups corn kernels, fresh or frozen
1 1/2	cups long grain white rice
3	or 4 scallions, chopped

Heat the oil in a large saucepan and add the onion, garlic, and chile. Sauté for about 4 minutes. Add the tomatoes and seasonings and cook for 4 to 5 minutes more over medium heat until the mixture thickens. Add the squash, water, corn, rice, and scallions and bring to a boil. Cover and cook for 15 to 20 minutes until the squash and rice are tender.

Remove from the heat and let stand for 10 to 15 minutes before serving. Serve with braised spinach or steamed broccoli.

Yield: 4 servings

Italian Garden Risotto

Italians are famous for their fruitful gardens. My late grand-father once grew a cucumber the size of a large watermelon; I think he brought the seeds from Sicily. This primavera-style risotto was inspired by the cascading Italian vegetables and herbs I have known (and grown).

1 1/2	tablespoons olive oil
1	small red onion, chopped
1	green bell pepper, seeded and diced
1	small zucchini or other summer squash, diced
1	cup diced eggplant
2	cloves garlic, minced
2	large tomatoes, diced
1 1/2	cups arborio rice
4 1/2	cups hot water
2	to 3 tablespoons chopped fresh parsley
1/2	teaspoon salt
1/2	teaspoon ground black pepper
1/4	cup grated Parmesan or Romano cheese
2	to 3 tablespoons chopped fresh basil (optional)

Heat the oil in a saucepan and add the onion, pepper, zucchini, eggplant, and garlic. Cook for 7 to 9 minutes over medium heat, stirring frequently. Add the tomatoes and cook for about 2 minutes more. Stir in the rice, 2 1/2 cups water, and seasonings. Cook (uncovered) over low heat for 10 minutes, stirring frequently. Gradually stir in the remaining 2 cups water and cook for 10 to 12 minutes more, continuing to stir, until the rice is tender. Remove from the heat and stir in the Parmesan cheese and basil. Let stand for a few minutes before serving.

Yield: 4 to 6 servings

Eggplant Dirty Rice

This dish pays homage to a Louisiana classic, dirty rice. Despite its name, this meal looks quite appealing. For this healthful meat-free variation, eggplant replaces the chicken. The vigorous spicing is the spirit of Cajun and Creole cooking.

1 1/2 tablespoons canola oil
1 medium yellow onion, diced
1 green bell pepper, seeded and diced
1 cup diced celery
2 cups diced eggplant
2 cloves garlic, minced
1 cup tomato sauce
2 tablespoons dried parsley
2 teaspoons dried oregano
1 teaspoon dried thyme
1/2 teaspoon salt
1/4 teaspoon ground cayenne
3 cups hot water
1 1/2 cups long grain white rice or wild pecan rice
1 (15-ounce) can red kidney beans, drained
1 bunch broccoli, cut into florets

In a large saucepan, heat the oil and add the onion, bell pepper, celery, eggplant, and garlic. Cook over medium heat for about 10 minutes, stirring frequently. Add the tomato sauce and seasonings and cook for 3 to 4 minutes more. Add the water, rice, and beans and bring to a boil. Cover the pan and cook for about 20 minutes, until the rice is tender.

Fluff the rice and stir in the broccoli. Let stand for 10 minutes before serving.

Yield: 4 servings

Rice Advice
Pass a bottle of Tabasco or other hot sauce at the table.

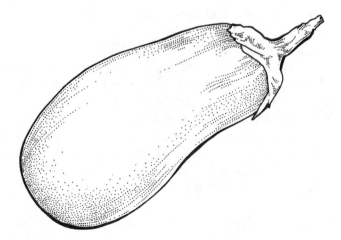

Squash Risotto with Escarole

Autumn squash, with their melding textures and mild flavors, are perfect for risotto. Escarole, a leafy green lettuce prized in Italian cooking, contributes a spinachlike taste.

1	tablespoon olive oil
1	medium yellow onion, chopped
10	to 12 mushrooms, sliced
2	cloves garlic, minced
2	cups peeled, diced butternut squash or red kuri squash
1½	cups arborio rice
4½	cups hot water
½	teaspoon ground white pepper
½	teaspoon salt
2	cups chopped fresh escarole or spinach
¼	cup diced roasted sweet peppers (canned or jarred variety)
¼	cup plus 2 tablespoons grated Parmesan cheese

Heat the oil in a large saucepan and add the onion, mushrooms, and garlic. Sauté for about 7 minutes. Add the squash, rice, 2½ cups water, and seasonings. Cook (uncovered) over low heat for about 10 minutes, stirring frequently.

Stir in the remaining 2 cups water, escarole, and roasted peppers. Cook for 10 to 12 minutes more, continuing to stir, until the rice is tender. Turn off the heat and fold in the cheese. Let stand for a few minutes before serving.

Serve the risotto with warm Italian bread.

Yield: 4 to 6 servings

Vegetarian Rice Cuisine

Festive Squash and Sweet Pea Risotto

This risotto is resplendent with convivial colors and flavors. You can use almost any winter squash for the preparation; red kuri and calabaza are two of my favorites.

1	tablespoon olive oil
1	medium onion, finely chopped
2	cloves garlic, minced
2	tomatoes, chopped
2	cups peeled, diced butternut, red kuri squash, or calabaza
1 1/2	cups arborio rice
4 1/2	cups hot water
1/2	teaspoon ground white pepper
1/2	teaspoon salt
1 1/2	cups green peas, fresh or frozen
1/4	cup plus 2 tablespoons grated Parmesan or Romano cheese

Heat the oil in a large saucepan and add the onion and garlic. Sauté for about 4 minutes. Stir in the tomatoes and sauté for 2 minutes more. Stir in the squash, rice, 2 1/2 cups water, and seasonings. Cook (uncovered) over low heat for about 10 minutes, stirring frequently.

Gradually stir in the remaining 2 cups water and peas and cook for 10 to 12 minutes more, continuing to stir, until the rice and squash are tender.

Remove from the heat and stir in the cheese. Let stand for a few minutes before serving. Serve with warm bread.

Yield: 6 servings

Verdant Risotto with Asparagus and Rapini

Rapini, also called broccoli rabe, is a leafy green vegetable with miniature broccoli florets. It has a blunt, mustardlike flavor and warmly complements the regal asparagus. To balance rapini's sharp flavors, I recommend using Pecorino Romano, which has a slightly stronger flavor than Parmesan. This is sort of an Italian version of Mexican Arroz Verde.

1	tablespoon olive oil
1	medium yellow onion, chopped
2	cloves garlic, minced
1½	cups arborio rice
4	cups hot water
½	cup dry white wine
½	teaspoon ground white pepper
½	teaspoon salt
10	to 12 asparagus spears, trimmed and cut into 1-inch sections
1	small bunch rapini (broccoli rabe) rinsed, stems removed, and coarsely chopped
2	tablespoons chopped fresh parsley (or 1 tablespoon dried)
¼	cup plus 2 tablespoons grated Romano cheese

Heat the oil in a large saucepan and add the onion and garlic. Sauté for about 4 minutes. Add the rice, 2 cups water, wine, and seasonings. Cook (uncovered) over low heat for about 10 minutes, stirring frequently.

Stir in the remaining 2 cups water, asparagus, rapini, and parsley. Cook for 10 to 12 minutes more, continuing to stir, until the rice is tender.

Remove from the heat and stir in the cheese. Let stand for a few minutes before serving. Serve with warm Italian bread.

Yield: 4 servings

Rice Advice

If rapini is unavailable, try 3 to 4 cups of chopped fresh spinach or escarole.

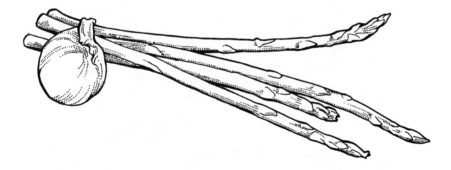

Beet Root Risotto

Rarely does a dish make me speechless, but the first bite of this dazzling pink risotto came oh so very close. After many tries I successfully arranged the marriage of beets with risotto. The union is sublime.

3	or 4 medium beet roots, scrubbed
1	tablespoon olive oil or canola oil
1	medium red onion, finely chopped
2	cloves garlic, minced
1 1/2	cups arborio rice
4	cups hot water
1/2	cup dry white wine
1/2	teaspoon ground white or black pepper
1/2	teaspoon salt
2	tablespoons chopped fresh parsley
1/4	cup plus 2 tablespoons grated Romano cheese

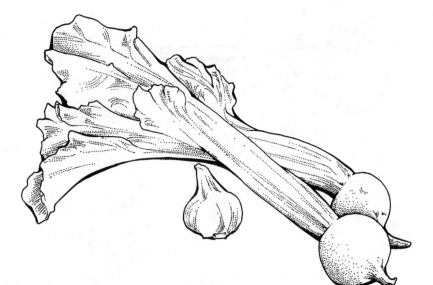

Preheat the oven to 375° F.

Wrap the beets in aluminum foil and place in a baking pan. Roast for 45 to 50 minutes, until the beets are tender. Remove the beets from the oven, unwrap, and let cool for a few minutes. Peel off the skin and dice the beets.

Heat the oil in a large saucepan and add the onion and garlic. Sauté for about 4 minutes. Add the rice, 2 cups water, wine, and dried seasonings. Cook (uncovered) over low heat for about 10 minutes, stirring frequently.

Stir in the beets, the remaining 2 cups water, and the parsley and cook for 10 to 12 minutes more, continuing to stir, until the rice is tender. Remove from the heat and stir in the cheese. Let stand for a few minutes before serving.

Serve the risotto with a tossed green salad.

Yield: 4 servings

Rice Advice

If the beet leaves are crisp and without blemishes, chop them and add to the risotto along with the beets. They taste like Swiss chard and offer a nice contrast of colors.

Sun-Dried Tomato and White Bean Risotto

Sun-dried tomatoes deliver a robust tomato essence while white beans lend a fortifying presence. This is a good midwinter risotto to make, especially when fresh juicy tomatoes are a distant memory and dried tomatoes must fill the void.

1	cup sun-dried tomatoes
1	tablespoon olive oil
1	small red onion, chopped
12	ounces mushrooms, sliced
2	cloves garlic, minced
2	tablespoons minced shallots
1 1/2	cups arborio rice
4	cups hot water
1/2	cup dry white wine or champagne
1 1/2	tablespoons dried parsley
1/2	teaspoon ground sage
1/2	teaspoon ground white pepper
1/2	teaspoon salt
1	(15-ounce) can cannellini beans, drained
1/4	cup plus 2 tablespoons grated Parmesan or Romano cheese

Soak the dried tomatoes in warm water for 30 minutes to 1 hour. Drain, discarding the liquid. Coarsely chop the tomatoes.

Heat the oil in a large saucepan and add the onion, mushrooms, garlic, and shallots. Cook for about 7 to 9 minutes over medium heat, stirring frequently. Add the tomatoes, rice, 2 cups water, wine, and seasonings. Cook (uncovered) over low heat for about 10 minutes, stirring frequently.

Gradually stir in the remaining 2 cups water and the beans and cook for 10 to 12 minutes more, continuing to stir, until the rice is tender. Remove from the heat and stir in the cheese. Let stand for a few minutes before serving.

Serve the risotto with warm bread.

Yield: 4 to 6 servings

Champagne, Mushroom, and Spinach Risotto

This risotto was inspired by one of the first sauces I ever created as a professional chef. Made with champagne, shallots, mushrooms, and a hint of tomato, the sauce offers an enticing combination of sultry flavors. Have the ingredients reappear together in the guise of a risotto, and the results are equally as satisfying.

1	tablespoon olive oil
1	small yellow onion, chopped
2	tablespoons minced shallots
12	ounces mushrooms, sliced
1	tablespoon tomato paste
1 1/2	cups arborio rice
3 1/2	cups hot water
1	cup dry champagne
1	teaspoon ground paprika
1/2	teaspoon ground black pepper
1/2	teaspoon salt
4	cups coarsely chopped fresh spinach
1/4	cup plus 2 tablespoons grated Parmesan or Romano cheese

Heat the oil in a large saucepan and add the onion, shallots, and mushrooms. Cook for 7 to 10 minutes over medium heat, stirring frequently. Stir in the tomato paste and cook for 1 minute over low heat. Stir in the rice, 2 cups water, champagne, and seasonings. Cook (uncovered) over low heat for about 10 minutes, stirring frequently.

Stir in the remaining 1 1/2 cups water and the spinach and cook for 10 to 12 minutes more, continuing to stir, until the rice is tender. Remove from the heat and stir in the cheese. Let stand for a few minutes before serving.

Serve the risotto with a tossed salad, warm bread, and a bottle of chilled champagne.

Yield: 4 servings

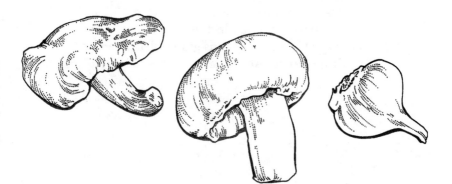

Summer Grill Risotto

Grilling aficionados will surely appreciate this summery risotto. The glory is in the vegetables: smoky, outdoorsy, and teeming with flame-invoked flavors. Creamy risotto proves to be a welcome medium for this adventurous medley.

2	green or red bell peppers
1	medium zucchini, cut into thirds lengthwise
12	ounces mushrooms
1	tablespoon olive oil
1	small red onion, chopped
2	cloves garlic, minced
1 1/2	cups arborio rice
4 1/2	cups hot water
2	or 3 tablespoons chopped fresh parsley
3/4	teaspoon salt
1/2	teaspoon ground black pepper
1/4	cup plus 2 tablespoons grated Parmesan or Romano cheese

Preheat the grill until the coals are ashen gray to white.

Place the bell peppers, zucchini, and mushrooms on the lightly oiled grill. Cook the vegetables on each side for 7 to 10 minutes, until grid-marked and tender. Remove the vegetables as they become done and place in a shallow bowl. Discard any charred spots and seeds and coarsely chop the vegetables. (Leave the small mushrooms whole).

Meanwhile, heat the oil in a saucepan and add the onion and garlic. Sauté for about 4 minutes. Stir in the grilled vegetables, rice, 2 1/2 cups water, and seasonings and cook over low heat for 10 minutes, stirring frequently. Gradually stir in the remaining 2 cups water and cook for 10 to 12 minutes more over low heat, continuing to stir, until the rice is tender.

Remove from the heat and stir in the Parmesan cheese. Let stand for a few minutes before serving. Serve with toasted garlic bread.

Yield: 6 servings

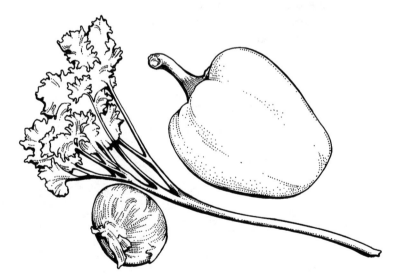

West Indian Pilau

Pilau is the Caribbean cousin to Middle Eastern pilaf. Here, a meatless pilau is fortified with mushrooms, West Indian pumpkin (or butternut squash), and legumes. Pilau is especially popular in Trinadad and Tobago.

1 1/2 tablespoons canola oil
1   medium yellow onion, diced
12   ounces mushrooms, sliced
2   cloves garlic, minced
1   jalapeño pepper, seeded and minced (optional)
2   cups hot water
2   cups peeled, diced West Indian pumpkin or winter
       squash
1 1/2 cups long grain white rice or parboiled rice
1   cup light coconut milk
2   tablespoons dried parsley
1   teaspoon dried thyme
1/2   teaspoon ground black pepper
1/2   teaspoon salt
1/4   teaspoon ground turmeric
1   cup cooked or canned pigeon peas or field peas,
       heated
2   large scallions, chopped

Heat the oil in a saucepan and add the onion, mushrooms, garlic, and jalapeño. Cook over medium heat for 7 to 8 minutes, stirring frequently. Stir in the water, pumpkin, rice, coconut milk, and seasonings and bring to a boil. Cover and cook over low heat for 18 to 20 minutes until the pumpkin is tender.

Fluff the rice and stir in the peas and scallions. Let stand on the stove top for about 10 minutes before serving.

Yield: 4 to 6 servings

Rice Advice

If coconut milk is too rich for your palate, try rice milk or water. Rice milk is available in natural food stores and well-stocked supermarkets.

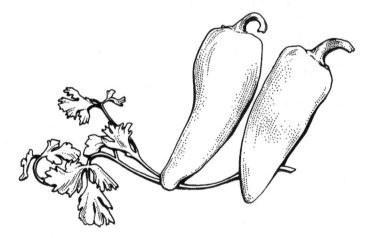

Vegetable Biryani

Biryani, an Indian version of paella, is a festive party dish prepared with a variety of vegetables and spices. Unlike many casseroles (which are subdued by monotone flavors and textures) this dish is a culinary adventure packed with alluring tastes.

1	tablespoon canola oil
1	medium yellow onion, diced
1	small zucchini, diced
2	cloves garlic, minced
1	large tomato, diced
2	teaspoons curry powder
1/2	teaspoon ground fenugreek
1/2	teaspoon garam masala
1/4	teaspoon ground cayenne pepper
1/4	teaspoon ground turmeric
3/4	teaspoon salt
3 1/4	cups hot water
1 1/2	cups brown basmati or long grain brown rice
2	large carrots, peeled and diced
1	small bunch broccoli, cut into florets
1	cup green peas, fresh or frozen

Preheat the oven to 375° F.

In a large cast-iron skillet or Dutch oven, heat the oil and add the onion, zucchini, and garlic. Cook over medium heat for 5 to 7 minutes, stirring frequently. Stir in the tomato and seasonings and cook for 1 minute more. Stir in the water, rice, and carrots. Cover the pan and place in the oven. Bake for 35 to 45 minutes, until the rice is tender.

Remove the pan from the oven and blend in the broccoli and peas while fluffing the rice. Cover the dish and return to the oven but turn off the heat; let stand for 5 to 10 minutes.

Serve with Cucumber Herb Raita (page 166) and/or Peach and Apple Chutney (page 167).

Yield: 4 to 6 servings

Rice Advice

Fenugreek and garam masala are available in the spice section of Indian markets, natural food stores, and well-stocked supermarkets. If you do not have garam masala, try adding ¼ teaspoon each of ground cumin and coriander and a scant touch of ground cloves. There is no substitute for fenugreek.

Southwestern Black Bean Stew with Cilantro Rice

Early in my culinary career I gravitated toward the sunny flavors of the American Southwest. When I finally visited New Mexico, it was more of a pilgrimage than a vacation. This dish invokes the vibrant, sizzling flavors of the Southwestern palate: cilantro, black beans, corn, chiles, and assertive spices.

1 1/2	cups long grain white rice or brown rice
3	cups hot water
2	to 3 tablespoons chopped fresh cilantro
1	tablespoon canola oil
1	medium onion, diced
1	red or green bell pepper, seeded and diced
1	small zucchini, diced
2	cloves garlic, minced
1	Red Fresno or jalapeño pepper, seeded and minced
2	(15-ounce) cans black beans, drained
1	(14-ounce) can stewed tomatoes
1	cup corn, fresh or frozen
2	teaspoons dried oregano
1 1/2	teaspoons ground cumin
1/2	teaspoon salt
1/2	teaspoon ground black pepper

Combine the rice and water in a saucepan and bring to a boil. Cover and cook over low heat for 15 to 20 minutes until the rice is tender. (For brown rice, cook for about 40 minutes and add about 1/2 cup more water). Fluff the rice and fold in the cilantro. Set aside and keep warm.

Meanwhile, heat the oil in another saucepan and add the onion, bell pepper, zucchini, garlic, and chile. Cook for 8 to 10 minutes over medium heat, stirring frequently. Stir in the beans, tomatoes, corn, and seasonings and cook for 10 to 15 minutes, stirring occasionally.

Spoon the cilantro-rice into shallow bowls and ladle the black bean stew over the top.

Yield: 4 to 6 servings

Rice Advice

The Red Fresno chile is similar to a red jalapeño only it has wider shoulders and a touch more heat.

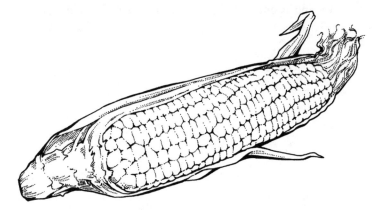

Teriyaki Vegetable Stir-Fry

During my college years I discovered the versatility of stir-fries. On weekends there was always a waiting line for the house wok. Almost any combination of vegetables can be rapidly stir-fried and blended with (or served over) steaming rice. For an authentic presentation, julienne the vegetables by cutting them into long narrow strips.

2	teaspoons canola oil
1	medium Japanese purple eggplant, julienned
1	red or yellow bell pepper, julienned
8	to 10 mushrooms, sliced
2	cloves garlic, minced
1	(2-inch) section of daikon, julienned
8	small broccoli florets
6	to 8 small bok choy leaves or pat soi, chopped
4	scallions, chopped
3	to 4 tablespoons light teriyaki sauce
1	teaspoon sesame oil
1	teaspoon bottled hot sauce or hot sesame oil
3	cups cooked short grain white or brown rice

Heat the oil in a large nonstick skillet or wok and add the eggplant, pepper, mushrooms, garlic, and daikon. Stir-fry for about 7 minutes. Stir in the broccoli, bok choy, and scallions and stir-fry for 2 minutes more. Stir in the teriyaki sauce, sesame oil, and hot sauce and lower the heat. Fold in the cooked rice and cook until the rice is steaming.

Spoon the mixture onto warm plates and serve hot.

Yield: 3 to 4 servings

Rice Advice

Pat soi, sometimes called tat soi, is a tender leafy green similar to bok choy. For diversity, try adding a few teaspoons of an Asian condiment such as oyster sauce, hoisin sauce, Thai peanut sauce, soy sauce, or ketchap manis, an Indonesian sweetened soy sauce.

Stove-Top Vegetable Pilaf

This pilaf is filled with nourishing, good-for-you vegetables. For a satisfying supper, serve with a side of steamed broccoli, asparagus, or spinach.

1	tablespoon canola oil
1	small yellow onion, chopped
8	to 10 mushrooms, sliced
1	green or red bell pepper, seeded and diced
1	small zucchini, diced
2	cloves garlic, minced
3	cups hot water
1 1/2	cups white long grain rice
2	carrots, peeled and sliced
2	tablespoons chopped fresh parsley (or 1 tablespoon dried)
1/2	teaspoon ground black pepper
1/2	to 1 teaspoon salt
1	(15-ounce) can black beans, red kidney beans, or other kind of beans, drained and warmed

Heat the oil in a saucepan and add the onion, mushrooms, pepper, zucchini, and garlic. Sauté for 5 to 7 minutes. Add the water, rice, carrots, and seasonings and bring to a boil. Cover and cook over low heat for 15 to 20 minutes until the rice is tender.

Fluff the rice and stir in the beans. Let stand for 5 to 10 minutes before serving.

Yield: 4 servings

Rice Advice

If you wish to make a whole grain pilaf with either brown rice, brown basmati, or Wehani, cook for about 40 minutes and add about 1/2 cup more water.

West African Jollof Rice

Jollof rice is a vibrant "party dish" served at celebrations and festive gatherings throughout West Africa. I have adapted it for the vegetarian palate, incorporating a bounty of vegetables and leafy greens.

1	tablespoon canola oil
1	medium onion, chopped
1	green bell pepper, seeded and diced
1	tablespoon minced fresh ginger root
1	jalapeño pepper, seeded and minced (optional)
2	large tomatoes, diced
2	to 3 teaspoons curry powder
2	teaspoons dried thyme leaves
1/2	teaspoon ground black pepper
1/2	teaspoon salt
1 1/2	cups long grain white rice or parboiled rice
3	cups hot water
2	large carrots, peeled and diced
1	tablespoon tomato paste
2	cups chopped greens (spinach, collard, or dande-lion greens)
1	(15-ounce) can black-eyed peas, drained

Heat the oil in a large saucepan and add the onion, bell pepper, ginger, and jalapeño. Sauté for about 7 minutes. Add the tomatoes and seasonings and sauté for about 2 minutes more. Stir in the rice, water, carrots, and tomato paste and bring to a boil. Cover and cook over low heat for about 15 minutes.

Stir in the spinach and peas and cook for about 5 minutes more. Fluff the rice and let stand for 10 minutes before serving.

Serve with Roasted Sweet Plantains (page 176).

Yield: 4 servings

Middle Eastern Vermicelli Pilaf

This toasty dish of rice and noodles is a celebrated Middle Eastern entrée. For years my grandmother served vermicelli pilaf every Sunday. I've updated it slightly by removing the chicken and butter and adding a few more vegetables.

8	ounces uncooked vermicelli or angel hair pasta
2	tablespoons canola oil
1	tablespoon olive oil
1	medium yellow onion, finely chopped
1	medium summer squash, diced
1	green or red bell pepper, seeded and diced
4	cups hot water
1¹/₂	cups long grain white rice or parboiled rice
1	(15-ounce) can chickpeas, drained
¹/₂	teaspoon ground turmeric
¹/₂	teaspoon ground black pepper
¹/₂	teaspoon ground cumin
1	teaspoon salt

Break up the vermicelli into small pieces. (This can be done over a large bowl with your hands).

Heat the canola oil in a large, deep skillet and add the vermicelli. Roast the noodles over medium heat for about 10 minutes, stirring frequently. Remove the pan from the heat when the noodles are golden brown.

Meanwhile, heat the olive oil in another large saucepan and add the onion, squash, and bell pepper. Sauté for about 7 minutes, until the vegetables are tender. Stir in the water, rice, chickpeas, seasonings, and roasted vermicelli and bring to a boil. Cover the pan and cook over low heat for 15 to 20 minutes until all of the liquid is absorbed.

Fluff the pilaf and let stand for 5 to 10 minutes before serving. If you'd like to serve an accompaniment, offer Sofrito (page 164).

Yield: 6 to 8 servings

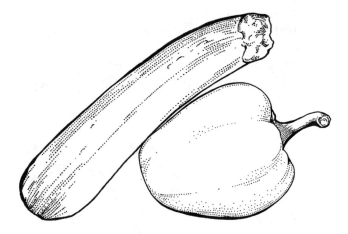

Roasted Pumpkin with Autumn Pilaf

Pumpkin, when baked whole and stuffed with pilaf, makes a grand centerpiece. For those who thought pumpkin was limited to pies and Halloween porch ornaments, this meal will prove enlightening.

1	(5- to 6-pound) whole pumpkin or red kuri squash
1	tablespoon canola oil
1	medium red onion, diced
1	red or green bell pepper, seeded and diced
1	small jalapeño pepper, seeded and minced
1	small zucchini, diced
1 1/2	cups long grain brown rice or brown basmati
1/2	teaspoon ground black pepper
1/2	teaspoon salt
1/4	teaspoon ground turmeric
3 1/4	cups hot water
8	to 10 broccoli florets, blanched
2	tablespoons minced fresh cilantro or parsley (optional)

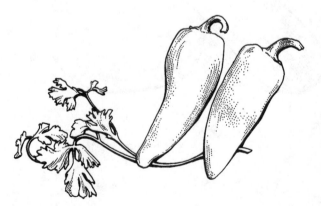

Vegetarian Rice Cuisine

Preheat the oven to 375° F.

With a sharp knife, cut a 4-inch lid off the top of the pumpkin. With a large spoon, scoop out the seeds and stringy fibers; discard or save for another use. Cover the hollowed-out center of the pumpkin with a sheet of foil and set the pumpkin lid back on top. Place in a baking pan filled with 1/2 inch of water and bake for 50 minutes to 1 hour until the inside is tender. Remove from the heat and keep warm.

Meanwhile, make the pilaf. Heat the oil in a saucepan and add the onion, peppers, and zucchini. Sauté for about 7 minutes until the vegetables are tender. Stir in the rice and seasonings and cook for 1 minute more. Add the water and bring to a boil. Cover and cook for about 40 minutes over low heat until the rice is tender.

Fluff the pilaf and stir in the broccoli and herbs. Spoon the pilaf into the center of the pumpkin and cover with the lid. (Discard the foil.) Present the pumpkin on a large platter in the center of the table. When serving the pilaf, scrape the inside of the pumpkin with a spoon and mix into the rice.

Yield: 4 servings

Rice Advice

You may also stuff two baked butternut squash with the pilaf filling.

Nasi Goreng

Nasi Goreng is Indonesian fried rice. Ketchap manis, a sweetened version of soy sauce, gives the rice a husky, molasseslike flavor. For a taste of an authentic Indonesian meal, serve Nasi Goreng with sambal, an Indonesian sweet-and-spicy condiment.

1	tablespoon canola oil
1	medium yellow onion, finely chopped
8	to 10 mushrooms, sliced
2	tablespoons minced shallots
1	or 2 jalapeño or serrano peppers, seeded and minced
2	medium tomatoes, diced
1	teaspoon paprika
4	cups cooked long grain white rice or basmati rice
8	broccoli florets, blanched
2	to 3 tablespoons ketchap manis
1	cucumber, peeled and finely chopped

Heat the oil in a skillet and add the onion, mushrooms, shallots, and chiles. Sauté for about 3 minutes. Add the tomatoes and paprika and sauté for 4 minutes more until the vegetables are tender. Stir in the rice, broccoli, and ketchap manis and cook over medium heat, stirring continuously, until the rice is steaming.

Place the cucumber in a serving bowl. Spoon the fried rice onto serving plates and top with the cucumber. Pass a bottle of ketchap manis and sambal at the table.

Yield: 4 servings

Rice Advice

Look for ketchap manis and sambal in well-stocked Asian markets. If ketchap manis is unavailable, try blending 2 tablespoons of light soy sauce with 2 teaspoons molasses or brown sugar.

Artichoke Lover's Pilaf

Accented with a hint of lemon, this tangy, delectable pilaf is a showcase for the wondrous artichoke.

1	tablespoon olive oil
1	medium yellow onion, diced
1	green or red bell pepper, seeded and diced
1	small zucchini or summer squash, diced
2	cloves garlic, minced
1 1/2	cups long grain white rice or parboiled rice
3	cups hot water
1	(14-ounce) can artichoke hearts, rinsed, drained, and coarsely chopped (about 6 hearts quartered)
1/4	cup chopped fresh parsley (or 2 tablespoons dried)
1/2	teaspoon ground black pepper
1/2	teaspoon salt
3	or 4 scallions, chopped
	Juice of 1 or 2 lemons

Heat the oil in a saucepan and add the onion, bell pepper, squash, and garlic. Sauté for about 7 minutes. Stir in the rice, water, artichokes, and seasonings and bring to a boil. Cover and cook for 15 to 20 minutes over low heat until the rice is tender.

Fluff the rice and blend in the scallions and lemon juice. Let stand for 5 to 10 minutes before serving. Serve the pilaf with a green vegetable such as asparagus, green beans, or braised spinach.

Yield: 4 servings

Pesto Risotto

Risotto and pesto were made for each other; the combination is a match made in heaven. The pesto can be made a day ahead of time.

1	tablespoon olive oil
1	small red onion, chopped
1	small yellow summer squash, diced
10	to 12 mushrooms, sliced
2	cups Arborio rice
4 1/2	cups hot water
1/2	cup dry white wine
6	to 8 asparagus spears or 12 green beans, coarsely chopped
1	cup Spinach Pesto (page 173) or Arugula Basil Pesto (page 174)

Heat the oil in a saucepan and add the onion, squash, and mushrooms. Cook for 7 to 9 minutes over medium heat, stirring frequently. Stir in the rice, 2 1/2 cups water, and wine. Cook (uncovered) over low heat for 10 minutes, stirring frequently. Gradually stir in the remaining 2 cups of water, add the asparagus, and cook for 10 to 12 minutes more, continuing to stir, until the rice is tender.

Remove from the heat and stir in the pesto. Let stand for a few minutes before serving. Serve with warm Italian bread.

Yield: 6 servings

Chilean Grand Bean and Rice Stew

This is an adaptation of a rustic vegetable stew called poro-tos granados ("choice beans") in Chile. It is a nourishing supper of pumpkin, corn, and beans and is typically served over (or cooked with) rice.

1	tablespoon canola oil
1	medium yellow onion, diced
1	green or red bell pepper, seeded and diced
2	or 3 cloves garlic, minced
2	large tomatoes, diced
1	tablespoon paprika
1	tablespoon dried oregano
1	tablespoon dried parsley
1	teaspoon ground cumin
3/4	teaspoon salt
1/2	teaspoon ground black pepper
2	cups peeled, diced pumpkin or other winter squash
2 1/4	cups hot water
1 1/2	cups corn kernels, fresh or frozen
1	cup long grain white rice or parboiled rice
1	(15-ounce) can cranberry beans or red kidney beans, drained

Heat the oil in a large saucepan and add the onion, bell pepper, and garlic. Sauté for about 5 minutes. Add the tomatoes and seasonings and cook for 3 to 4 minutes more, stirring frequently. Add the pumpkin and water and bring to a boil. Stir in the corn and rice, cover, and cook for 15 to 20 minutes over low heat, until the pumpkin and rice are tender.

Fluff the rice and stir in the beans. Let stand for 10 minutes before serving.

Yield: 4 servings

Rice Advice

Butternut squash, red kuri, or hubbard squash may be substituted for pumpkin. Other kinds of beans may also be used.

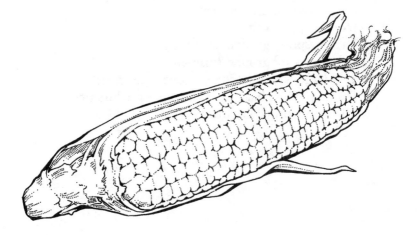

Savory Sambar Rice

Sambar is a Sri Lankan lentil and vegetable curry. The scent of fresh ginger pervades this vibrantly spiced stew. For a deep curry flavor, use Madras curry or another quality curry powder imported from India. A yogurt condiment such as Cucumber Herb Raita (page 166) makes a cooling accompaniment.

1/2	cup green or red lentils, rinsed
6	cups water
1	tablespoon canola oil
1	medium yellow onion, diced
1	green or red bell pepper, seeded and diced
2	teaspoons minced fresh ginger root
1	large tomato, diced
2	teaspoons Madras or other quality curry powder
1/2	teaspoon ground fenugreek
3/4	teaspoon salt
1/4	teaspoon ground cayenne pepper
1/4	teaspoon ground turmeric
1	large white potato, scrubbed and diced
1/2	cup white basmati or long grain white rice
10	or 12 broccoli florets

Place the lentils and water in a saucepan and cook for about 45 minutes until tender. Drain, reserving 2 1/2 cups of the cooking liquid.

Heat the oil in another saucepan and add the onion, bell pepper, and ginger. Sauté for about 5 minutes. Stir in the tomato and seasonings and cook for about 1 minute more. Add the lentils, cooking liquid, potato, and rice and bring to a boil. Reduce the heat to low and cook for 20 to 25 minutes over low heat until the potatoes are tender, stirring occasionally. Stir in the broccoli and cook for 5 to 10 minutes more.

Serve with Cucumber Herb Raita (page 166).

Yield: 4 servings

Rice Advice
Fenugreek is available in the spice section of Indian markets, natural food stores, and well-stocked supermarkets. While there is no real substitute for fenugreek, if it is unavailable add another aromatic spice such as cumin or coriander.

Jay's Vegetable Jambalaya

This meatless jambalaya was one of the all-time best sellers at my restaurant in Ithaca, New York. Jambalaya embodies the feisty spirit of Cajun and Creole cooking. The penetrating herbs and spices leave a pleasing "roundness" in the mouth, and the vegetables acquire a rustic flavor.

1½ cups long grain brown rice, white rice, or wild pecan rice
3 cups hot water
1½ tablespoons canola oil
1 green bell pepper, seeded and diced
1 small yellow onion, diced
1 small eggplant or zucchini, diced
8 to 10 mushrooms, sliced
3 cups Piquant Creole Sauce (page 165)
10 to 12 broccoli florets
1 cup cooked or canned red kidney beans (optional)

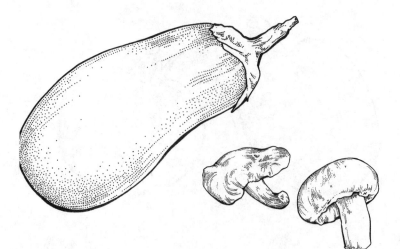

Combine the rice and water in a saucepan and bring to a boil. Cover and cook over low heat for 15 to 20 minutes (about 40 minutes for brown rice). Set aside for 10 minutes. (This can be done a day ahead of time.)

Heat the oil in a saucepan and add the bell pepper, onion, eggplant, and mushrooms. Cook over medium heat for about 10 minutes, stirring frequently. Add the Creole Sauce and bring to a simmer. Reduce the heat to low and fold in the cooked rice, broccoli, and beans. Cook for 5 to 10 minutes more, stirring frequently.

Serve the jambalaya with corn bread and pass a bottle of Tabasco sauce at the table. If you'd like, sprinkle shredded provolone cheese over the top before serving.

Yield: 4 to 6 servings

Rice Advice

You can make the Piquant Creole Sauce a few days ahead of time. If you are using brown rice, you may want to add 1/2 cup more water to the pot.

Red Hot Lava Stir-Fry

Years ago I discovered a fiery red Asian condiment called chili-garlic paste. This searing, pungent (and addicting) sauce became one of my favorite ways to reinvigorate and perk up a stir-fry. You can moderate the degree of heat by altering the amount of chili-garlic paste you pour in.

2 teaspoons canola oil
1 medium Japanese purple eggplant (or small Italian eggplant), halved and julienned
1 red or yellow bell pepper, julienned
2 large scallions, chopped
1/4 pound extra-firm tofu, diced
4 ounces water chestnuts, drained
2 ounces snow peas
2 teaspoons minced fresh ginger root
3 tablespoons light soy sauce
1 teaspoon hot sesame oil
1 to 4 teaspoons chili-garlic paste or Scotch bonnet pepper sauce
8 small broccoli florets
1 (8-ounce) can tomato sauce
3 cups cooked long grain white or brown rice, heated

Heat the oil in a large nonstick skillet or wok and add the eggplant and pepper. Stir-fry for about 5 minutes. Add the scallions, tofu, water chestnuts, snow peas, and ginger and fry for 1 minute more. Stir in the soy sauce, sesame oil, and chili-garlic paste and stir-fry for 3 minutes more. Add the broccoli and stir-fry for 2 minutes more.

Lower the heat and stir in the tomato sauce; simmer for 5 to 7 minutes, stirring frequently. Place the rice on warm plates and spoon the vegetables and red sauce over the top. Let the rice soak up the sauce. (You may also fold the cooked rice into the stir-fry mixture.) Serve with a cool beverage.

Yield: 2 to 3 servings

Rice Advice

Chili-garlic paste is available in Asian markets and in the specialty condiment section of well-stocked supermarkets. If you are an incendiary maniac, add two or three Thai chile peppers or serrano peppers to the dish while it cooks.

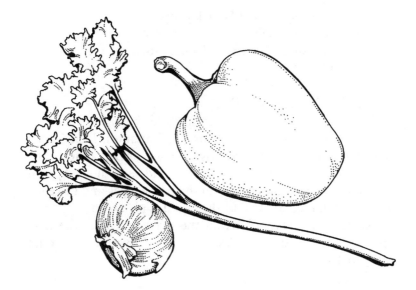

Rice and Sweet Potato au Gratin

This hearth-style casserole can be served as a main entrée or a side dish, depending on your needs and appetite. Sweet potatoes add a nice dose of beta carotene as well as a sweet starchy flavor.

1	tablespoon canola oil
1	medium yellow onion, diced
1	green or red bell pepper, seeded and diced
1	small zucchini, diced
2	cloves garlic, minced
1	medium bunch broccoli, cut into florets
4½	cups hot water
2	cups long grain white rice or parboiled rice
2	cups diced sweet potatoes
¼	cup chopped fresh parsley (or 2 tablespoons dried)
1	teaspoon ground black pepper
1	teaspoon salt
1	cup shredded lowfat Swiss, mozzarella, or provolone cheese

Preheat the oven to 375° F.

Heat the oil in a large skillet and add the onion, bell pepper, zucchini, and garlic. Sauté for 5 to 7 minutes. Transfer the vegetables to a 9-by-13-inch casserole dish or Dutch oven. Stir in the broccoli, water, rice, potatoes, and seasonings. Spread the rice and vegetables evenly in the pan. Cover and bake for 25 to 30 minutes until all of the liquid is absorbed.

Remove the casserole from the oven and fluff the rice. Sprinkle the cheese evenly over the top. Cover and let stand for 5 to 10 minutes before serving.

Yield: 6 to 8 servings

Vegetable Rice Burrito

On the drawing board a burrito is a neat tidy meal wrapped in a tortilla. The fun begins when you tear into the wrapping and the filling oozes out; burritos are a pleasure to eat. For this meatless version, the vegetables can be varied; try mixing in diced eggplant, green peas, blanched broccoli, or black beans—whatever your heart desires.

1	tablespoon canola oil
1	green or red bell pepper, seeded and diced
1	small zucchini, diced
8	to 10 mushrooms, sliced
2	cups cooked white rice or brown rice
1	cup cooked or canned red kidney beans or black beans
1	cup corn kernels, fresh or frozen
2	tablespoons chopped fresh parsley (or 1 tablespoon dried)
1/2	teaspoon ground cumin
1/2	teaspoon ground black pepper
1/2	teaspoon salt
1/2	cup shredded lowfat Swiss or Monterey jack cheese
4	(10-inch) flour tortillas

Heat the oil in a large nonstick skillet and add the pepper, zucchini, and mushrooms. Sauté for 5 to 7 minutes. Stir in the rice, beans, corn, and seasonings and cook for 4 to 6 minutes over medium heat, stirring frequently, until the rice is steaming. Remove from the heat and fold in the cheese.

Warm the tortillas over a burner or in a hot pan and place on serving plates. Spoon the rice and bean mixture into the centers. Roll the tortillas around the filling, creating burritos. Serve with Smoky Chipotle Salsa (page 175) or one of your favorite salsas.

Yield: 4 servings

Country Garden Paella

Paella comes from the Catalan term for *"frying pan."*
*Although paella served in the Spanish countryside includes
seafood or meat, I've adapted it for the meatless kitchen.
This vegetarian version is filled with a harvest of garden
vegetables.*

1	tablespoon olive oil
1	medium yellow onion, diced
1	medium zucchini, diced, or 2 cups diced eggplant
1	red or orange bell pepper, seeded and diced
1	large tomato, diced
2	cloves garlic, minced
3 1/4	cups hot water
1 1/2	cups short or medium grain Valencia or arborio rice
2	cups chopped fresh spinach, kale, or escarole
1	cup green peas, fresh or frozen
1/4	cup minced fresh parsley (or 2 tablespoons dried)
1	teaspoon dried thyme
1/2	teaspoon ground black pepper
1/2	teaspoon salt
1/4	teaspoon ground turmeric

Preheat the oven to 375° F.

In a large cast-iron skillet or Dutch oven, heat the oil and add the onion, zucchini (or eggplant), bell pepper, tomato, and garlic. Sauté for 5 to 7 minutes. Stir in the water, rice, greens, peas, and seasonings. Cover and place in the oven; bake for 18 to 20 minutes until the rice is tender. Remove the skillet from the oven and fluff the rice. Let stand for 10 minutes before serving.

Place the skillet in the center of the table and serve hot.

Yield: 4 servings

Rice Advice

Valencia rice is grown in the Valencia region of Spain and is the preferred grain for paella. Saffron is an expensive spice that gives paella its authentic yellow tint, but I use the more widely available (and less costly) turmeric.

Wild Rice Paella with Asparagus and Corn

This whole grain paella makes a splendid centerpiece for special occasions and holiday events. Chunks of corn on the cob are stewed with the rice and instill a lusty, savage quality. (A version of this dish first appeared in a Thanksgiving article I wrote for the Vegetarian Times.)

1	tablespoon olive oil or canola oil
2	cups sliced leeks
1	medium zucchini, diced
3	or 4 cloves garlic, minced
4½	cups hot water
1½	cups medium grain brown rice
½	cup wild rice
2	medium carrots, peeled and diced
1	cup green peas, fresh or frozen
2	cobs of corn, shucked and cut into 1-inch sections
2	tablespoons minced fresh parsley (or 1 tablespoon dried)
1	teaspoon dried thyme
½	teaspoon ground black pepper
½	teaspoon ground turmeric
½	teaspoon salt
12	asparagus stalks, fibrous ends removed

Preheat the oven to 375° F.

In a large cast-iron skillet or Dutch oven, heat the oil and add the leeks, zucchini, and garlic. Cook over medium heat for about 7 minutes, stirring occasionally. Stir in the water, both rices, carrots, peas, corn, and seasonings and cover. Place in the oven and bake for about 45 minutes.

Remove the skillet from the oven and fluff the rice. Arrange the asparagus over the top and cover. Bake for 5 minutes more until all of the liquid is absorbed. Remove from the heat and let stand for 10 minutes.

Place the skillet in the center of the table and serve hot.

Yield: 4 to 6 servings

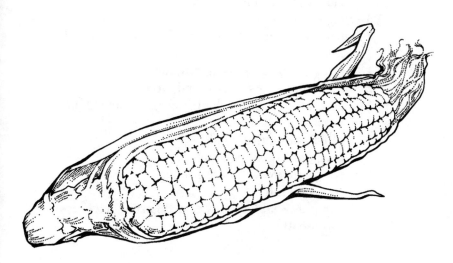

Puerto Rican Vegetable Asopao

Asopao is a Puerto Rican dish similar to paella, but soupier. This meatless version is a delicious melange of vegetables, plantains, herbs, and rice.

1 1/2 tablespoons canola oil
1 medium onion, diced
1 green or red bell pepper, seeded and diced
1 small eggplant, diced (about 2 cups)
1 yellow plantain, peeled and cut into 1-inch sections
2 cloves garlic, minced
3 1/2 cups hot water
1 1/4 cups Valencia, arborio, or other short grain white rice
1 (14-ounce) can stewed tomatoes
2 medium carrots, peeled and diced
1 1/2 cups green peas, fresh or frozen, or canned pigeon peas
1 tablespoon dried parsley
2 teaspoons dried oregano
1/2 teaspoon ground black pepper
1/2 teaspoon salt
1/4 cup plus 2 tablespoons grated Parmesan cheese (optional)

Heat the oil in a large saucepan and add the onion, bell pepper, eggplant, plantain, and garlic. Cook for 8 to 10 minutes over medium heat, stirring frequently. Add the water, rice, tomatoes, carrots, peas, and seasonings. Cook over low heat for about 25 minutes, stirring occasionally. Stir in the Parmesan cheese and set aside for 5 to 10 minutes before serving.

Serve the asopao in large shallow bowls.

Yield: 6 servings

Rice Advice

Asopao can also contain 1 or 2 tablespoons of capers and/or a fresh herb called recaito, which has a mild cilantro-like flavor. Pigeon peas, also called gandules or gungo peas, are small round beans prevalent in Caribbean cooking.

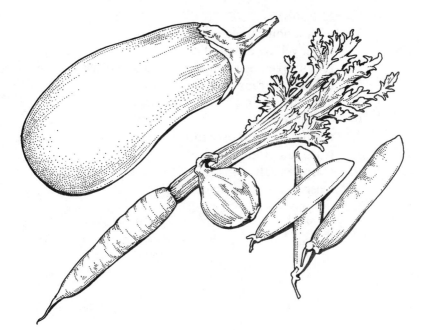

Yellow Rice and Black Beans

Black beans and rice are the dynamic duo of Latin American cooking. In Cuba they are called moros y cristianos (for Moors and Christians). In Central America, they are called frijoles y arroz and referred to as casamiento, or "married." This colorful version is one of my favorites.

For the rice:
1   tablespoon olive oil
1   small yellow onion, chopped
3   cups hot water
1 1/2 cups long grain white rice, Texmati, or parboiled rice
1/2   teaspoon ground turmeric
1/2   teaspoon salt

For the beans:
1   tablespoon canola oil
1   small yellow onion, diced
1   red or green bell pepper, seeded and diced
2   (15-ounce) cans black beans, drained
1   (14-ounce) can stewed tomatoes
1/4   cup dark rum
2   teaspoons dried oregano
1   teaspoon ground cumin
1/2   teaspoon salt
1/2   teaspoon ground black pepper

To make the rice, heat the oil in a saucepan and add the onion. Sauté for 3 to 4 minutes. Stir in the water, rice, and seasonings and bring to a boil. Cover and cook for 15 to 20 minutes over low heat. Remove from the heat and fluff the rice.

Meanwhile, prepare the beans. Heat the oil in a saucepan and add the onion and bell pepper. Sauté for 5 minutes. Stir in the beans, tomatoes, rum, and seasonings and cook for 12 to 15 minutes over medium heat, stirring occasionally.

Spoon the cooked yellow rice into shallow bowls and ladle the black beans over the top. To round out this vivid color scheme, serve a green or red vegetable on the side.

Yield: 4 servings

Rice Advice

For diversity, add either a minced chile pepper, chopped fresh herbs, chopped garlic, or chopped ginger to the rice or the beans. If you wish to use brown rice, add about ½ cup more water and cook the rice for about 40 minutes.

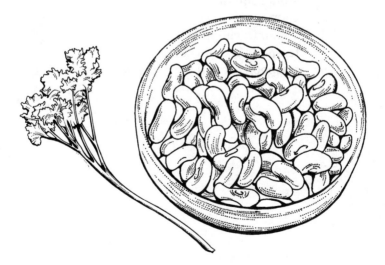

Jessica's Black Rice and Pumpkin Stew

My friend Jessica Robin traveled throughout Indonesia and Thailand on bicycle and came back with wild tales about her culinary adventures. This was one of the exotic dishes I was able to re-create. The sweetly flavored black rice cuts (and complements) the spiciness of the pumpkin stew.

3 1/2 cups hot water
1 1/4 cups black rice, Wehani, or black rice blend
2 tablespoons shredded coconut
2 tablespoons fresh chopped cilantro
1 1/2 to 2 tablespoons ketchap manis or light soy sauce
1 tablespoon canola oil
1 medium yellow onion, diced
2 tablespoons minced shallots
1 Thai or red serrano chile, seeded and minced
4 cups peeled, diced pumpkin, butternut, or other winter squash
3 cups water
4 scallions, chopped
1 teaspoon ground cumin
1/2 teaspoon ground black pepper

Combine the hot water, rice, and coconut in a saucepan and bring to a boil. Cover and cook for 35 to 40 minutes over low heat until the rice is tender. Stir in the cilantro and soy sauce and set aside for about 10 minutes.

Meanwhile, heat the oil in another saucepan and add the onion, shallots, and chile. Sauté for about 4 minutes. Add the squash, water, scallions, and seasonings and bring to a boil. Cook over low-medium heat for about 20 minutes, stirring occasionally, until the squash is tender. Set aside until the rice is done.

Spoon the cooked rice into the center of shallow serving bowls or plates and ladle the pumpkin stew over the top. Serve with sambal or hot sauce on the side.

Yield: 4 servings

Rice Advice

Black rice and ketchap manis are available in well-stocked Asian markets. If you don't have ketchap manis, add 1 or 2 teaspoons of molasses to the rice with the soy sauce. Medium grain brown rice can also be used.

Chapter 5

Rice Companions

Condiments and Accompaniments

Although most of the dishes in *Vegetarian Rice Cuisine* are cooked and combined with a meal's worth of flavors, occasionally one craves a little something extra, perhaps a light sauce or condiment on the side for diversity's sake. A variety of accompaniments can embellish and adorn rice meals while providing last-minute surges of flavor. These accompaniments intensify, complement, and coax out the meal's optimal flavors.

This chapter offers a cross section of some of the most inviting companions for rice dishes. Most are culturally linked to rice, such as Puerto Rican Sofrito, Thai Panang Curry, and Indonesian Peanut Sauce. Piquant Creole Sauce forms the basis of jambalaya, one of the flagship dishes of Louisiana cuisine. Smoky Chipotle Salsa, Roasted Sweet Plantains, and Red Lentil Dal frequently appear on the same plate with rice in equatorial dishes throughout the world.

These rice companions bring welcome flavors to the table.

Sofrito

Sofrito is a condiment found on Puerto Rican and Spanish tables. It is spooned over rice dishes for a last-minute flavor boost.

1	tablespoon canola oil
1	medium onion, diced
1	green bell pepper, seeded and diced
2	cloves garlic, minced
1	(15-ounce) can stewed tomatoes
1/2	teaspoon ground cumin
1/2	teaspoon ground black pepper
1/2	teaspoon salt
2	tablespoons chopped fresh cilantro

Heat the oil in a saucepan and add the onion, bell pepper, and garlic. Sauté for 5 to 7 minutes. Add the tomatoes and dry seasonings and bring to a simmer. Cook for 8 to 10 minutes more over low heat, stirring frequently. Stir in the cilantro and remove from the heat. Serve the sofrito with a variety of rice dinners. The sauce will keep for 3 or 4 days if refrigerated.

Yield: 6 servings

Rice Advice

If you happen to come across a fresh herb called *recaito*, add it to the sauce in place of cilantro. It has a mild cilantro-like flavor and is prominently used in Puerto Rican cooking.

Piquant Creole Sauce

This classic sauce is healthful, hearty, and exuberantly spiced. The "holy trinity" of Creole cooking—bell peppers, onions, and celery—forms the basis of the sauce and a battalion of peppery spices delivers a blast of well-rounded heat.

1   tablespoon canola oil
1   green bell pepper, seeded and diced
1   medium onion, diced
2   stalks celery, sliced
2   cloves garlic, minced
1   (16-ounce) can crushed tomatoes (about 2 cups)
1/2   cup water
2   teaspoons dried oregano
1 1/2 teaspoons dried thyme
1   teaspoon Tabasco or other bottled hot sauce
1/2   teaspoon salt
1/2   teaspoon ground black pepper
1/4   teaspoon ground white pepper
1/8   teaspoon ground cayenne pepper

Heat the oil in a saucepan and add the bell pepper, onion, celery, and garlic. Cook over medium heat for 8 to 10 minutes, stirring frequently. Add the crushed tomatoes, water, and seasonings. Cook over medium-low heat for about 20 minutes, stirring occasionally. The sauce can be refrigerated for later. Spoon the sauce over mild rice for an infusion of flavor. This sauce is the pillar of Jay's Vegetable Jambalaya (page 146).

Yield: About 3 cups

Cucumber Herb Raita

Raita is a cooling Indian yogurt condiment. It makes a calming accompaniment to spicy rice dishes and curries. A variety of fresh garden herbs can be used.

> 2 cups lowfat plain yogurt
> 1 medium cucumber, chopped (peeled, if waxed)
> 2 or 3 tablespoons chopped fresh mint, cilantro, or parsley

Combine all of the ingredients in a mixing bowl. Cover and chill for at least 1 hour. Serve cold.

Serve on the side of curries and other spicy rice dishes.

Yield: 6 to 8 servings

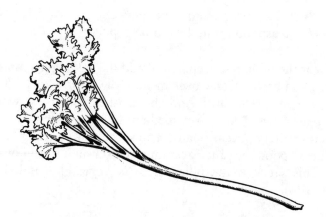

Peach and Apple Chutney

Chutney is a fruity, sweet-and-tart condiment rooted in Indian and Caribbean cooking. Mango chutney is by far the most common chutney, but almost any fruit can be used. This peach and apple rendition is one of my favorites to make, especially after visiting a local orchard.

1	medium yellow onion, diced
4	ripe peaches, diced (unpeeled)
4	apples, diced (unpeeled)
1	cup red wine vinegar
1	cup apple cider
1/2	cup raisins
1/2	cup brown sugar
3	or 4 cloves garlic, minced
1	tablespoon minced fresh ginger root
1	teaspoon ground cumin
1/2	teaspoon ground black pepper
1/2	teaspoon salt
1/4	teaspoon ground cloves

Combine all of the ingredients in a large, nonreactive saucepan. Cook over medium-low heat for 45 minutes to 1 hour, stirring occasionally, until the mixture is chunky and jamlike. Remove from the heat and let cool to room temperature, then chill. Reheat and serve with a variety of rice dishes.

Yield: 4 cups

Thai Panang Curry Sauce

Thai curries are exquisite blends of coconut milk, fresh herbs, and pungent pastes. There are several kinds of curry pastes on the market, including red, green, and yellow varieties; some are hotter than others. Panang is my favorite.

1	tablespoon canola oil
1	small onion, chopped
1	clove garlic, minced
2	teaspoons Thai curry paste (preferably panang curry)
1	(14-ounce) can light coconut milk
2	tablespoons light soy sauce
	Juice of ½ lime
1	tablespoon cornstarch
1	tablespoon warm water
2	tablespoons chopped fresh cilantro or basil (when in season)

Heat the oil in a saucepan and add the onion and garlic. Sauté for 2 to 3 minutes. Stir in the curry paste and cook for about 1 minute more over low heat, stirring frequently. Stir in the coconut milk, soy sauce, and lime juice and cook over low-medium heat for about 5 minutes until it begins to simmer.

Meanwhile, combine the cornstarch and water in a small bowl, forming a slurry. When the sauce begins to simmer, gradually whisk the slurry into the sauce and cook for 1 to 2 minutes more, stirring frequently. The sauce should thicken slightly. Stir in the fresh herbs and remove from the heat. Spoon the sauce over mild rice dishes, Indian curries, and stir-fries.

Yield: 8 to 10 servings (about 2 cups)

Rice Advice

Thai curry pastes, once hard to find, are now readily available in most well-stocked supermarkets and Asian grocery stores.

Red Lentil Dal

Dal is a well-cooked Indian curry usually made with lentils or other legumes. When properly cooked and spiced, the lentils should dissolve in one's mouth. Dal makes a lively companion to most basmati and jasmine rice dishes.

1	tablespoon canola oil
1	medium onion, chopped
2	cloves garlic, minced
1	jalapeño pepper, seeded and minced (optional)
1/2	teaspoon ground turmeric
1/2	teaspoon ground cumin
1/2	teaspoon garam masala (or ground coriander)
1/4	teaspoon ground black pepper
1	cup red lentils, rinsed
4	cups hot water
2	cups diced sweet potatoes or white potatoes
1	teaspoon salt

Heat the oil in a saucepan and add the onion, garlic, and jalapeño. Sauté for about 5 minutes. Stir in the seasonings (except the salt) and cook for 1 minute more. Stir in the lentils and water and bring to a boil. Add the potatoes and cook over low heat for 50 minutes to 1 hour, stirring occasionally, until the lentils are tender. Stir in the salt and let stand for 10 minutes.

Serve the dal with a variety of basmati and jasmine rice dishes.

Yield: 8 to 12 servings

Rice Advice

Red lentils are available in well-stocked grocery stores and Indian markets. Green lentils or yellow split peas may be substituted. Garam masala can be found in the spice section of Indian markets, natural food stores, and well-stocked grocery stores.

Indonesian Peanut Sauce

This rich, scrumptious sauce has a nutty, aromatic flavor.

1	tablespoon peanut oil or canola oil
1	small red onion, chopped
2	cloves garlic, minced
1	serrano or other hot chile pepper, seeded and minced
1	tablespoon minced fresh ginger
6	tablespoons chunky peanut butter
1	cup light coconut milk
1/4	cup hot water
3	tablespoons ketchap manis (or 3 tablespoons light soy sauce sweetened with 1 tablespoon molasses)
1 1/2	tablespoons fresh lime juice
2	tablespoons minced fresh cilantro or Thai basil

Heat the oil in a saucepan and add the onion, garlic, chile, and ginger. Sauté for 3 minutes. Blend in the peanut butter, coconut milk, water, ketchap manis, lime juice, and herbs. Bring the sauce to a simmer over medium heat, stirring frequently.

Remove from the heat and serve over stir-fries and mild rice dishes.

Yield: 6 to 8 servings

Rice Advice

Ketchap manis is available in well-stocked Asian markets. For a citrusy nuance, add 2 teaspoons minced lemongrass along with the sautéed ingredients. Lemongrass is a brittle, lemon-scented herb available in Asian markets and specialty produce sections of large grocery stores.

Cranberry Chutney

Cranberry chutney is a dynamic alternative to those insipid cans of cranberry relish served on so many holiday tables. It makes a colorful complement to pilafs, curries, and pilaus.

12   ounces fresh or frozen cranberries
1   large apple, diced (do not peel)
1   large pear, diced (do not peel)
1   large onion, diced
4   cloves garlic, minced
1   tablespoon minced fresh ginger root
3/4   cup brown sugar
1/2   cup raisins, or 1 cup chopped dried apricots
1 1/2 cups red wine vinegar
1   cup apple juice or apple cider
1/2   teaspoon ground black pepper
1/2   teaspoon ground cumin
1/2   teaspoon salt
1/4   teaspoon ground cloves

Combine all of the ingredients in a large, nonreactive saucepan. Cook over low heat, stirring occasionally, for 25 to 30 minutes until the mixture has a jamlike consistency. Allow the chutney to cool to room temperature. Serve immediately or refrigerate for later. If refrigerated, the chutney should keep for several weeks.

Yield: 6 to 8 servings

Spinach Pesto

Indeed, the world would be a sorry place without pesto. The scent of fresh pesto does for the appetite what the scent of a rose does for romance. In this verdant version, spinach adds valuable nutrients and flavor to the cherished basil venue.

4	cloves garlic
1/2	cup diced walnuts, pine nuts, or unsalted cashews
2	juicy plum tomatoes, diced
2	cups packed fresh spinach leaves
1	cup packed fresh basil leaves
1/3	cup olive oil
1/2	teaspoon salt
1/2	teaspoon ground black pepper
1/2	cup grated Parmesan cheese

Place the garlic, nuts, and tomatoes in a food processor fitted with a steel blade or in a blender. Process for 10 seconds, stopping once to scrape the sides. Add the spinach, basil, oil, and seasonings and process for 10 to 15 seconds more, until smooth. Stop at least once to scrape the sides. Transfer to a mixing bowl and fold in the cheese. Refrigerate until ready to use.

Yield: About 2 1/4 cups

Rice Advice
Adding tomatoes to the pesto eliminates some of the oil, thereby reducing the overall fat content.

Arugula Basil Pesto

Peppery arugula and summery basil team up for another inspired pesto. They are both easy plants to grow, even under the care of a neophyte gardener such as myself. This pesto reinvigorates rice salads, risotto, and entrées.

4	cloves garlic
1/4	cup pine nuts, walnuts, or unsalted cashews
2	juicy plum tomatoes, diced
1	cup packed fresh basil leaves
1	cup packed fresh arugula leaves
1/4	cup olive oil
1/2	teaspoon salt
1/2	teaspoon ground black pepper
1/4	cup grated Parmesan cheese

Place the garlic and nuts in a food processor fitted with a steel blade or in a blender. Process for 10 seconds, stopping once to scrape the sides. Add the tomatoes, basil, arugula, oil, and seasonings and process for 10 to 15 seconds more, until smooth. Stop at least once to scrape the sides. Transfer to a mixing bowl and fold in the cheese. Refrigerate until ready to use.

Yield: About 1 1/2 cups

Rice Advice
Adding tomatoes to the pesto reduces the overall oil (and fat) content.

Smoky Chipotle Salsa

If you are hooked on salsa, you'll savor this smoldering chipotle-infused variation. This salsa complements a variety of rice entrées, including Vegetable Rice Burrito (page 151), Breakfast Black Bean and Rice Burrito (page 188), and Arroz Verde (page 105).

2	large tomatoes, diced
1	green or red bell pepper, seeded and diced
1	small yellow onion, diced
1	large clove garlic, minced
1	to 2 chipotle peppers, chopped
2	tablespoons chopped fresh cilantro
	Juice of 1 lime
1 1/2	teaspoons dried oregano
1	teaspoon ground cumin
1/2	teaspoon salt
1/4	teaspoon ground black pepper
1	(16-ounce) can crushed tomatoes

Combine all of the ingredients (except the crushed tomatoes) in a large bowl and mix well. Place three-quarters of the mixture in a food processor fitted with a steel blade (or in a blender) and process/pulse for 5 to 10 seconds, creating a chunky vegetable mash.

Return the mash to the bowl and blend in the crushed tomatoes. Wrap the salsa and chill for at least 1 hour, allowing the flavors to mingle. Stir the salsa before serving.

Yield: 3 cups (6 to 8 servings)

Rice Advice

Chipotle chiles are large jalapeño peppers that have been dried and smoked. They are available canned or air-packed in well-stocked supermarkets. If air-packed, they should be rehydrated in warm water for about 1 hour before using.

Roasted Sweet Plantains

Plantains are frequent plate mates with rice in African, Caribbean, and Latin American meals. I prefer plantains on the ripe, sweet, yellowish side. To ripen a green plantain, store it at room temperature for 5 to 7 days; it should gradually turn yellow and develop dark spots (like an overripe banana).

2   or 3 large yellow plantains
1/4 teaspoon ground nutmeg, allspice, or cinnamon

Preheat the oven to 400° F.

Cut off the tips of the plantains and place on a baking sheet. Bake for 15 to 20 minutes, until the skin is charred and puffy. Remove the plantains from the oven and let cool for a few minutes. Slice the plantains down the center lengthwise and peel back the skin. Cut the plantains in half widthwise, sprinkle with spices, and transfer to serving plates. Serve with a variety of rice entrées such as West African Jollof Rice (page 133), West Indian Pilau (page 124), or Chilean Grand Bean and Rice Stew (page 142).

Yield: 4 servings

Chapter 6

Breakfast and Brunch

Rice and Shine

Rice for breakfast makes perfect sense. Grains, after all, are what most breakfast cereals are made of—wheat, bran, oats, corn, and of course, rice. True, morning grains are in a processed form and do not require cooking (except oatmeal). But if you have "cooked rice" already in the kitchen, breakfast is a natural time to include it in a meal. Besides, rice provides a solid source of energy for the day to come.

This chapter offers a creative collection of morning dishes for the multifaceted grain. The recipes range from the traditional Central American breakfast of Gallo Pinto (rice and beans) to the original Pumpkin Rice Pancakes and Apple Molasses Rice Bowl.

Indonesian Fried Rice and Pineapple Fried Rice highlight the Southeast Asian–style breakfast while Maple Nut Rice Porridge is reminiscent of good old-fashioned oatmeal.

Whether it's breakfast or brunch, these morning rice dishes will pleasantly wake up your palate. You'll see that rice is right at home on the breakfast table.

Gallo Pinto

This morning rendition of rice and beans is the Costa Rican national dish. It will supply you with substantial energy for the day ahead. Gallo Pinto is traditionally served with Salsa Linzano, a condiment similar to Worcestershire sauce.

1	tablespoon canola oil
1	small onion, chopped
1	red bell pepper, seeded and diced
1	or 2 cloves garlic, minced
4	cups cooked long grain brown rice or white rice
1	(15-ounce) can black beans, drained
1	teaspoon dried oregano
1/2	teaspoon ground cumin
	About 2 teaspoons Worcestershire sauce
	Salt and ground black pepper, to taste

Heat the oil in a large nonstick skillet and add the onion, pepper, and garlic. Sauté for about 5 minutes. Add the cooked rice, beans, and seasonings and cook over medium heat about 10 minutes, stirring frequently, until the rice and beans are completely reheated. Stir in the Worcestershire sauce.

Spoon onto serving plates and season with salt and pepper to taste. Pass the bottle of Worcestershire sauce at the table.

Yield: 4 servings

Rice Advice
Salsa Linzano is available in Latin America markets and specialty "hot and spicy" stores.

Maple-Nut Rice Porridge

Move over oatmeal! Make room for this delicious brown-rice porridge! Maple syrup brings out the subtle sweetness and nuttiness of brown rice, nature's other hot morning grain.

2	cups cooked short grain or long grain brown rice
1½	cups lowfat milk or rice milk
¼	cup plus 2 tablespoons maple syrup
½	cup slivered almonds or chopped walnuts
⅓	cup raisins
¼	teaspoon ground cinnamon or nutmeg

Combine all of the ingredients in a saucepan and cook for 8 to 12 minutes over low heat, stirring frequently. Ladle into cereal bowls and serve hot. If you'd like, top with sliced bananas, strawberries, or other fresh fruit.

Yield: 4 servings

Rice Advice
Rice milk is available in natural food stores and in the health foods section of well-stocked supermarkets.

Apple-Molasses Rice Bowl

This fruity and comforting breakfast will perk up your spirits and tickle your morning palate. Molasses adds an earthy, unrefined sweetness.

2½ cups cooked medium grain brown rice or white rice
2 cups lowfat milk or rice milk
2 tablespoons dark molasses
1 tablespoon honey or maple syrup
2 apples, diced
½ cup slivered almonds or diced pecans
1 cinnamon stick (or ¼ teaspoon ground cinnamon)

Combine all of the ingredients in a saucepan. Cook for 10 to 15 minutes over low heat, stirring frequently. Remove the cinnamon stick and let the porridge cool for a few minutes before serving. Ladle into cereal bowls and serve warm.

Yield: 4 servings

Indonesian Fried Rice

In Indonesia, as in Central America, fried rice is often eaten for breakfast. This version is traditionally served with sambal, a sweet and spicy Indonesian hot sauce; fried rice will add a little spice to your morning routine.

1	tablespoon canola oil
1	small onion, chopped
1	red bell pepper, seeded and diced
1	jalapeño or other chile, seeded and minced
4	cups cooked white basmati or jasmine rice
1	to 2 tablespoons ketchap manis or light soy sauce
1	large egg, beaten (or 1 ounce egg substitute)
	Ground black pepper, to taste
1	small cucumber, chopped (optional)

Heat the oil in a large nonstick skillet and add the onion, pepper, and chile. Sauté for 5 to 7 minutes, until the vegetables are tender. Stir in the cooked rice and ketchap manis and cook over medium heat for about 7 minutes, stirring frequently, until the rice is steaming. Rapidly stir in the egg and cook until the egg reaches a scrambled consistency.

Season with black pepper at the table. If you'd like, spoon chopped cucumber over the top.

Yield: 4 servings

Rice Advice

Ketchap manis is a sweetened, syrupy Indonesian version of soy sauce. Look for ketchap manis and sambal in well-stocked Asian markets. If ketchap manis is unavailable, substitute 1 tablespoon light soy sauce mixed with 1 teaspoon molasses or brown sugar. (But ketchap manis is worth the hunt.)

Pumpkin-Rice Pancakes

When it comes to lumberjack breakfasts, pumpkin pancakes have become my signature dish. These amber-hued flapjacks are astonishingly tasty and offer an imaginative way to use leftover cooked rice.

1 1/2 cups unbleached all-purpose flour
1   teaspoon salt
1/4   cup sugar
2   teaspoons baking powder
1/2   teaspoon ground allspice or cinnamon
2   medium eggs, beaten (or the equivalent of egg substitute)
2   tablespoons canola oil
2   cups buttermilk, lowfat milk, or rice milk
1 1/2 cups cooked, mashed pumpkin or winter squash
1 1/2 cups cooked brown rice, Wehani rice, or wild rice

Combine the dry ingredients in a mixing bowl. In a separate bowl, whisk the eggs, oil, and milk together. Fold the liquid ingredients into the dry ingredients, forming a batter. Blend in the mashed pumpkin and rice.

Preheat a lightly greased nonstick griddle or skillet over moderately high heat. Spoon about 1 cup of the batter onto the griddle and spread to the edges of the pan. Flip the pancake after 3 to 4 minutes (when the edges turn brown). Continue cooking until the remaining side is golden brown. Remove to a warm serving plate and repeat the process with the remaining batter. Stack the finished pancakes and cover with wax paper.

Serve the pancakes with real maple syrup and serious coffee.

Yield: 6 to 8 pancakes

Spicy Corn Griddle Cakes

These spicy pancakes will serve as an alarm clock for your taste buds! They pack a wallop of flavor.

3/4 cup fine cornmeal
1/2 cup unbleached all-purpose flour
2 tablespoons sugar
1 teaspoon salt
1 teaspoon baking powder
1 medium egg, beaten (or 2 ounces egg substitute)
2 tablespoons canola oil
1 cup buttermilk, lowfat milk, or rice milk
1 cup cooked white rice or brown rice (preferably short grain)
1/2 cup cooked corn kernels, fresh or frozen
1 or 2 red Fresno or jalapeño chiles, seeded and minced

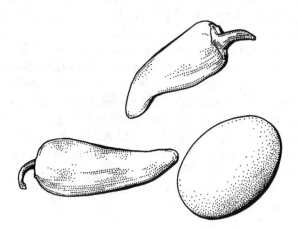

Combine the dry ingredients in a mixing bowl. In a separate bowl, whisk the egg, oil, and milk together. Fold the liquid ingredients into the dry ingredients, forming a batter. Blend in the rice, corn, and chiles.

Preheat a lightly greased nonstick griddle or skillet over moderately high heat. Spoon about 3/4 cup of the batter onto the griddle and spread to the edges of the pan. Flip the pancake after 3 to 4 minutes (when the edges turn brown). Continue cooking until the remaining side is light brown and then remove to a warm plate. Reduce the heat to medium and repeat the process with the remaining batter. Stack the finished pancakes and cover with wax paper.

Serve with a variety of accompaniments such as Smoky Chipotle Salsa (page 175), Sofrito (page 164), black beans, or guacamole.

Yield: About 4 pancakes

Rice Advice

For milder Cheesy Corn Griddle Cakes, add about 1/4 cup shredded lowfat Monterey jack or Swiss cheese to the batter and leave out the chiles.

Wild Rice and Pumpkin Muffins

Wild rice extends its culinary range in these wholesome, beta carotene–enriched pumpkin muffins.

1/2	cup canola oil
1	cup buttermilk, lowfat milk, or rice milk
1	cup brown sugar
2	large eggs (or 4 ounces egg substitute)
2	cups mashed pumpkin (about 1 (16-ounce) can)
1 1/2	cups cooked wild rice or Wehani rice
2	cups unbleached all-purpose flour
1/2	cup rolled oatmeal
2	teaspoons baking powder
1	teaspoon ground cinnamon
1/2	teaspoon salt

Preheat the oven to 375° F.

Whisk together the oil, buttermilk, sugar, and eggs in a mixing bowl, until the batter is creamy. Blend in the mashed pumpkin and wild rice.

Mix the dry ingredients in a separate bowl. Gently fold the dry ingredients into the liquid mixture and beat until completely incorporated. Spoon the batter into a lightly greased muffin tin (or paper muffin cups) and bake for about 50 minutes, until a toothpick inserted in the center comes out clean. Remove from the oven and let stand for about 15 minutes on a rack before serving.

Yield: 6 mega-muffins or about 12 small muffins

Rice Advice

Smaller muffins will take 5 to 10 minutes less time to bake.

Pineapple Fried Rice

This tropically flavored fried rice offers a fruity alternative to standard egg-and-meat versions. If you prefer a tamer meal in the morning, leave out the chili-garlic paste.

2	teaspoons canola oil
1	small red onion, chopped
1	red or green bell pepper, seeded and slivered
1	to 2 teaspoons minced fresh ginger root
4	cups cooked white or brown basmati or jasmine rice
1	cup diced pineapple, fresh or canned
3	tablespoons light soy sauce
1	to 2 teaspoons chili-garlic paste (optional)
2	tablespoons chopped fresh cilantro

Heat the oil in a large nonstick skillet or wok and add the onion, bell pepper, and ginger. Stir-fry over medium heat for 5 minutes. Stir in the cooked rice, pineapple, soy sauce, and chili-garlic paste. Stir-fry for 5 to 7 minutes more, until the rice is steaming. (Cook a few minutes more if you like the rice crispy.)

Fold in the cilantro and serve at once.

Yield: 2 or 3 servings

Rice Advice

Chili-garlic paste is available in Asian markets and well-stocked grocery stores.

Breakfast Black Bean and Rice Burrito

This bursting-at-the-seams burrito is a sizzling way to start the day. It certainly is an appealing healthful alternative to artery-clogging bacon and greasy home fries.

2	teaspoons canola oil
1/2	cup diced roasted sweet red pepper (about 1/2 bell pepper)
1	small zucchini, diced
4	scallions, chopped
2	cups cooked white rice or brown rice
1	cup cooked or canned black beans
2	tablespoons chopped fresh parsley (or 1 tablespoon dried)
1/2	teaspoon ground cumin
1/2	teaspoon ground black pepper
1/2	teaspoon salt
2	medium eggs, beaten (or 4 ounces egg substitute)
1/2	cup shredded lowfat Swiss or Monterey jack cheese
4	(10-inch) flour tortillas

Heat the oil in a large nonstick skillet and add the pepper, zucchini, and scallions. Sauté for 5 minutes. Stir in the rice, beans, and seasonings and cook for 3 to 4 minutes over medium heat. Rapidly blend in the eggs and cook for a few minutes more, stirring frequently. When the eggs are completely cooked, remove from the heat and fold in the cheese.

Warm the tortillas over a burner or in a pan and place on serving plates. Spoon the rice-and-bean mixture into the centers, forming logs. Roll the tortillas around the filling to form a burrito. Serve with Smoky Chipotle Salsa (page 175) or your favorite salsa or guacamole.

Yield: 4 servings

Zucchini Carrot Rice Muffins

These morning muffins have a secret ingredient: orange juice. The juice replaces about half of the oil, creating a lighter, moister muffin. The only problem is that you'll want to devour more than one!

1/2	cup orange juice
1/2	cup canola oil
1	cup brown sugar
2	large eggs, beaten (or 4 ounces egg substitute)
1	cup grated zucchini
1	cup peeled, grated carrot
2	cups unbleached all-purpose flour
1	tablespoon baking powder
1	teaspoon salt
1	teaspoon ground cinnamon
1	teaspoon ground nutmeg
1	cup cooked white rice or brown rice (preferably short grain)
1	cup raisins or diced walnuts

Preheat the oven to 350° F.

Whisk together the juice, oil, and sugar in a mixing bowl. Add the eggs and continue whisking until the batter is creamy. Fold in the zucchini and carrots. In a separate bowl, combine the flour, baking powder, salt, and spices. Fold the dry ingredients into the liquid ingredients, forming a batter. Fold in the rice and raisins.

Pour the batter into a lightly greased muffin tin and bake for about 30 minutes until a toothpick inserted in the center comes out clean. Remove from the heat and let cool for a few minutes before serving.

Yield: 12 muffins

Riz Cous Polenta

Polenta is a solid cornmeal cake served in various guises throughout the world. The addition of riz cous offers an opportunity to mix complementary grains. This also makes a welcome accompaniment to vegetarian chili and stews.

2¹/₂ cups water
¹/₂ teaspoon salt
¹/₄ teaspoon ground black pepper
¹/₂ cup fine yellow cornmeal
¹/₂ cup riz cous
1 cup corn kernels, fresh or frozen
¹/₄ cup chopped roasted red sweet peppers
¹/₄ cup plus 2 tablespoons grated Parmesan or
  Romano cheese
2 cups Sofrito (page 164) or 1 (15-ounce) can of
  your favorite tomato sauce, heated

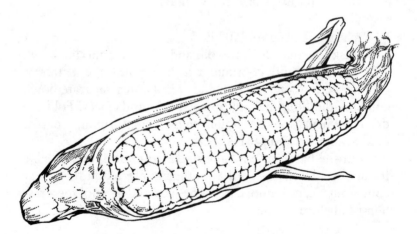

Combine the water, salt, and black pepper in a sturdy saucepan and bring to a boil. Lower the heat and gradually stir in the cornmeal and riz cous. Cook for 8 to 10 minutes over low heat, stirring frequently, until thick. Stir in the corn and roasted peppers and cook for 2 to 4 minutes more, continuing to stir.

Remove from the heat and fold in the cheese. Spread the polenta into a lightly greased 9-inch round pan. Let stand for 10 minutes before serving. (You may also refrigerate and reheat later.)

To serve, cut the polenta into wedges. Place the slices of polenta on serving plates and spoon the Sofrito or tomato sauce over the top.

Yield: 6 servings

Rice Advice

To avoid clumping, gradually stir the cornmeal and riz cous into the boiling water. Keep stirring until any lumps dissipate. Cook the polenta until a wooden spoon stands upright in the center of the pot.

Asparagus Rice Quiche with Herbes de Provence

In the eighties it seemed every restaurant on the planet offered quiche on the menu. It was too much. After years of abstinence, I finally invited quiche back into the culinary loop. This rice fortified version is scented with Herbes de Provence, a fragrant mixture of thyme, sage, basil, rosemary, oregano, lavender, and mint. In addition to its appealing flavor, this quiche is also lower in fat than most quiches of yore.

1	tablespoon canola oil
1	small red onion, diced
1	red or green bell pepper, seeded and diced
1	cup milk
4	ounces egg substitute (equivalent to 2 eggs beaten)
1	cup cooked short grain white rice or brown rice
1/2	to 1 cup shredded lowfat Swiss or cheddar cheese
10	to 12 asparagus spears, trimmed and cut into half-inch sections
4	scallions, chopped
1	to 2 teaspoons Herbes de Provence
1/2	teaspoon salt
1/2	teaspoon ground black pepper
1	(9-inch) deep-dish quiche crust or pie shell

Preheat the oven to 375° F.

Heat the oil in large nonstick skillet and add the onion and bell pepper. Sauté for about 4 minutes. Remove from the heat and let cool to room temperature.

Meanwhile, in a mixing bowl blend together the milk, eggs, rice, cheese, asparagus, scallions, herbs, and seasonings. Blend in the onions and peppers. Pour the egg-vegetable mixture into the quiche crust. Place the quiche on a baking pan and bake for 40 to 45 minutes until the center is firm and slightly brown. Remove from the oven and let stand for 15 minutes before serving. Serve with crusty French bread.

Yield: 6 servings

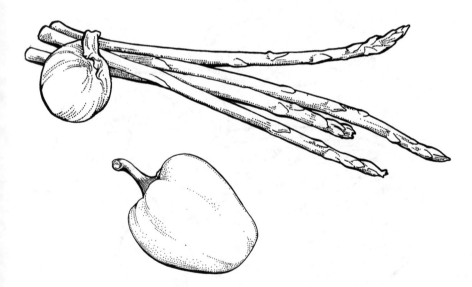

Chapter 7

Twice as Nice

Rice Puddings and
Light Delights

When I was growing up, rice pudding was a special treat if I behaved. I remember it as silky, creamy, studded with plump raisins, and dusted ever-so-lightly with nutmeg. Granted, it was from a local diner, but it was damn good rice pudding, well worth modifying my behavior.

It seems everyone has a favorite rice pudding recipe. Unfortunately, they often are loaded with heavy cream, eggs, or butter, all of which appear on the enemies list of a heart-smart diet. However, it is possible to create delectable and rewarding rice puddings without all the extra baggage and calories. Seasonal fruit, such as bananas, blueberries, and mangoes, can be added in place of the eggs. In place of heavy cream, try lowfat milk, soy milk, or rice milk. Rice pudding is just as satisfying when it's healthful.

In general, short grain rices such as arborio and sweet rice (or glutinous rice) are ideal for rice puddings and other desserts. (The shorter the grain, the more likely the grains will cling and stick together.) Rice has an affinity for coconut, and these are often paired together in desserts such as Mango Sticky Rice, Coconut Sweet Rice, and Black Rice Pudding. Rice also bonds well with chocolate, as exemplified by Chocolate Mocha Rice Delight.

The ability of rice to absorb flavors makes it a natural filler for cakes, muffins, and pies. Additionally, rice adds the "good" kind of carbohydrates (complex, not simple). Granted, eating a slice of Strawberry-Rhubarb Rice Pie or Carrot-Rice Spice Cake is still indulging (and rightly so!). But the presence of rice, albeit a small quantity, makes it a slightly better treat.

Coconut Sweet Rice

This Southeast Asian dessert has a creamy, porridgelike texture. To make this a "sweet rice light," replace half of the coconut milk with water or rice milk.

1 cup glutinous (sticky) rice
2 cups light coconut milk (or 1 cup rice milk and 1 cup coconut milk)
1/4 cup plus 2 tablespoons sugar

Soak the rice in plenty of water for 2 to 4 hours. Drain, discarding the water.

Combine the rice, water, and coconut milk in a sturdy saucepan. Cook over low heat for 20 to 25 minutes, stirring frequently. Remove from the heat and stir in the sugar. Let stand for 15 minutes. Serve as a warm dessert or chill for later. Garnish with sliced fresh fruit on the side.

Yield: 6 servings

Rice Advice

The traditional cooking method is to steam the rice until tender. If you have a predilection for coconut and chocolate, sprinkle about 1/4 cup semisweet chocolate chips over the chilled rice and microwave for about 30 seconds. It's scrumptious! Rice milk is available in natural food stores and in the health food section of well-stocked supermarkets.

Mango Sticky Rice

Patrons of Thai restaurants will recognize this exotic and tasty combination of rice and mango. Mangoes have a coral flesh and tropical fruit flavor with hints of pineapple, citrus, and peach.

1	cup glutinous (sticky) rice
1	cup hot water
1	cup light coconut milk or rice milk
1/4	cup plus 2 tablespoons sugar
2	tablespoons shredded coconut
1	or 2 large ripe mangoes, peeled, pitted, and sliced

Soak the rice in plenty of water for 2 to 4 hours. Drain, discarding the water.

Combine the rice, water, coconut milk, sugar, and grated coconut in a saucepan. Cook over low heat for 20 to 25 minutes, stirring frequently. Remove from the heat and let cool slightly. Refrigerate for about 1 hour.

Mold the rice in the center of 4 dessert plates and place the mango slices on the side.

Yield: 4 servings

Rice Advice

The easiest way to peel a mango is to pare it like a potato. Once peeled, cut as many slices as you can before hitting the stone-like pit. Scrape the remaining flesh around the pit. Only ripe, juicy mangoes will work for this dish; green (unripe mangoes) lack sweetness and flavor.

To make a perfect mound of rice, pack the rice in a small mold or custard-style bowl and invert onto the plate. If the rice sticks, lightly spray the bowl with a vegetable spray before packing.

Banana-Rum Rice Pudding

I prepared this banana lover's delight for Alive and
Wellness, *an alternative health show on the America's
Talking channel. Bananas, rum, and raisins harmonize
sweetly with rice.*

3	cups cooked white rice (preferably short grain)
2	cups lowfat milk or rice milk
1/4	cup sugar
1/2	cup raisins or currants
1/4	cup dark rum
2	bananas, peeled and mashed
1/2	teaspoon ground nutmeg
2	or 3 tablespoons chopped pistachio nuts (optional)

Combine all of the ingredients (except the nutmeg and
nuts) in a saucepan and cook for 15 to 20 minutes over low
heat, stirring frequently. Transfer the pudding to a large bowl
and chill for at least 1 hour before serving.

When you are ready to serve, spoon the rice pudding into
bowls and sprinkle with nutmeg. If you'd like, top with pis-
tachio nuts.

Yield: 6 servings

Blueberry-Mint Rice Pudding

Blueberries turn this rice pudding into a winsome treat with an inviting light purplish blue hue. Fresh mint cleanses the palate.

3	cups cooked short grain white rice or brown rice
2	cups lowfat milk or rice milk
1/4	cup plus 2 tablespoons sugar
2	cups blueberries, fresh or frozen
2	to 3 tablespoons chopped fresh mint
	Ground nutmeg or allspice (for garnishing)

Combine all of the ingredients in a saucepan (except the mint and nutmeg) and cook for 15 to 20 minutes over low heat, stirring frequently. Transfer the pudding to a large bowl and stir in the mint. Chill for at least 1 hour before serving.

When ready to serve, spoon the rice pudding into bowls and garnish with any extra mint leaves. Sprinkle nutmeg over the top.

Yield: 6 servings

Indian Rice Pudding (Kheer)

Cardamom and cinnamon contribute a warm lingering spice presence to this authentic Indian dessert.

3 cups lowfat milk or rice milk
1 1/2 cups cooked basmati rice or long grain white rice
1/2 cup sugar
1/4 cup raisins
2 to 3 tablespoons shredded coconut
1/4 teaspoon ground cardamom
1 cinnamon stick
1/4 cup slivered almonds

Combine all of the ingredients (except the almonds) in a saucepan and cook for 25 to 30 minutes over low heat, stirring occasionally. Transfer the mixture to a bowl and chill for 1 to 2 hours.

When you are ready to serve, remove the cinnamon stick and spoon the pudding into bowls. Sprinkle the almonds over the top.

Yield: 6 servings

Rice Advice
Cardamom is available in the spice section of Indian markets, natural food stores, and well-stocked supermarkets.

Arroz con Leche

Next to flan, rice pudding is one of the most treasured Mexican desserts. Arroz con Leche is imbued with delicate spices and discreet flavors. The peel (or zest) of citrus fruit adds a refreshing nuance.

2 1/2 cups lowfat milk or rice milk
2 cups cooked white rice (preferably short grain)
1/2 cup sugar
1/4 cup raisins
1/2 teaspoon vanilla extract
1 cinnamon stick
1 (2-inch) strip of lime or orange peel
2 to 3 tablespoons grated sweetened coconut (optional)

Combine all of the ingredients in a saucepan. Cook for 35 to 40 minutes over low heat, stirring occasionally, until the mixture thickens. Transfer the mixture to a serving bowl and chill 2 hours.

When you are ready to serve, remove the cinnamon stick and citrus peel and spoon the pudding into bowls. Garnish with a twist of lime or orange and sprinkle with coconut.

Yield: 6 servings

Black Rice Pudding

When combined with coconut milk and lowfat milk, black rice turns a deep, blackberry purple. Save this delicious treat for special occasions.

1   cup black rice or black rice blend
2¹/₂ cups water
1   cup light coconut milk
1   cup lowfat milk or rice milk
¹/₄ cup plus 2 tablespoons sugar
2   tablespoons grated coconut (optional)

Combine the rice and water in a saucepan. Cover and cook over low heat for about 40 minutes. Remove from the heat and let stand for 10 minutes. (The rice may be made up to a day ahead of time.)

When you are ready to make the pudding, combine the cooked rice, coconut milk, milk, and sugar in a saucepan. Cook over low heat for 30 minutes, stirring frequently. Remove from the heat and let cool slightly.

Transfer the pudding to a serving bowl and refrigerate for about 2 hours before serving. Garnish by sprinkling the shredded coconut over the top.

Yield: 6 to 8 servings

Chocolate Mocha Rice Delight

This luscious dessert incorporates one of my favorite ingredients, chocolate, the diva of desserts. It melts smoothly into the rice pudding and mesmerizes the taste buds with its familiar flavor.

3	cups cooked short grain white rice
2	cups vanilla soy milk, rice milk, or lowfat milk
1/4	cup Kahlua or other coffee liqueur
1/4	cup sugar
1	cup semisweet chocolate chips
2	or 3 tablespoons diced walnuts
6	to 8 fresh mint leaves (for garnishing)

Combine the rice, milk, coffee liqueur, and sugar in a saucepan. Cook for 15 to 20 minutes over low heat, stirring frequently. Stir in the chocolate chips and cook for about 1 minute more, until the chocolate melts completely into the pudding. Transfer to a serving bowl and chill for at least 1 hour before serving.

Spoon the pudding into bowls and sprinkle the walnuts over the top. Garnish with mint leaves.

Yield: 6 servings

Piña Colada Rice Pudding

The tropical flavors of mango and pineapple permeate this fun, island-inspired treat.

3	cups cooked short grain rice
1	cup light coconut milk
1	cup pineapple juice
1/2	cup sugar
1/4	cup currants or raisins
2	tablespoons dark rum
1/2	teaspoon ground nutmeg

Combine all of the ingredients (except the nutmeg) in a saucepan. Cook for 15 to 20 minutes over low heat, stirring frequently. Remove from the heat and chill for at least 1 hour before serving.

When you are ready to serve, spoon the pudding into bowls and sprinkle the nutmeg over the top. Garnish each bowl with a tiny paper umbrella or swizzle stick.

Yield: 6 servings

Strawberry-Rhubarb Rice Pie

The sight of strawberry-rhubarb pies at the farmers' market is a sure sign that summer has arrived. The addition of rice to the fruit filling results in a pie with a firm, dense texture; as a result, a slice doesn't ooze all over the plate.

2	cups diced fresh rhubarb
2	cups sliced fresh strawberries
1	cup brown sugar
1/4	cup apple juice
1	teaspoon fresh lime juice
1/2	teaspoon ground cinnamon
1/4	teaspoon ground cloves
2	tablespoons cornstarch
1	cup short grain white rice or brown rice
2	(9-inch) deep-dish pie shells

Preheat the oven to 375° F.

Combine the rhubarb, strawberries, sugar, apple juice, lime juice, and spices in a saucepan. Cook over low heat for 8 to 10 minutes, until the rhubarb dissolves into a thick mass. Remove from the heat and very gradually whisk in the cornstarch. (Whisk until any lumps disappear.) Whisk in the rice and set aside for about 5 minutes.

Pour the fruit mixture into one of the pie shells. Cover the pie with the remaining shell. Trim the edges and cut slits in the center of the lid to allow steam to escape. Place the pie on a baking pan and bake for 45 minutes to 1 hour, until the crust is golden brown. Remove from the oven and let cool to room temperature. Refrigerate for at least 1 hour before serving.

Yield: 6 to 8 servings

Carrot-Rice Spice Cake

I would like to say that this recipe came to me in a dream. Truthfully, it came while I was in the middle of making a carrot cake and contemplating what to do with some leftover rice. So in went the rice. The rice augmented the cake with crunchiness and won a thumbs-up from all who indulged.

1	cup canola oil
1/2	cup orange juice
2	cups sugar
2	large eggs, beaten
2	cups unbleached all-purpose flour
2	teaspoons ground cinnamon
2	teaspoons baking powder
3/4	teaspoon salt
2	cups peeled, grated carrot
1	cup diced walnuts
1	cup cooked white rice or brown rice (preferably short grain)
1	cup raisins, chopped dates, or chopped figs

Preheat the oven to 350° F.

Whisk together the oil, juice, and sugar in a mixing bowl. Add the eggs and continue whisking until the batter is creamy. In a separate bowl, combine the flour, cinnamon, baking powder, and salt. Fold the dry ingredients into the liquid ingredients, forming a batter. Fold in the carrots, walnuts, rice, and dried fruit.

Pour the batter into a lightly greased 9-inch cake pan or springform pan. Bake for about 1 hour until a toothpick inserted in the center comes out clean. Remove from the heat and let cool for several minutes before serving. If you'd like, ice the cake with Yogurt Cream Cheese Icing (recipe follows).

Yield: 1 cake (about 12 servings)

Yogurt Cream Cheese Icing

What's a carrot cake without cream cheese icing? Naked, that's what. This tangy topping calls for reduced-fat cream cheese and yogurt instead of regular cream cheese and butter.

1/4	cup plain lowfat yogurt
8	ounces lowfat or nonfat whipped cream cheese
6	ounces confectioners' sugar

With a mixing spoon blend all of the ingredients together until creamy. Refrigerate until ready to ice the cake.

Yield: Icing for 1 (9-inch) cake

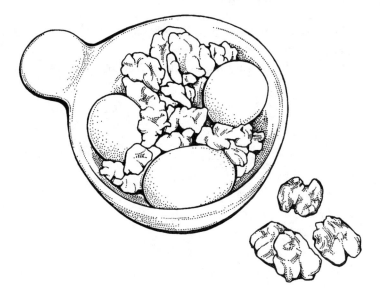

Banana-Nut Rice Bread

I am a prodigious banana eater. However, the fruit must fall within a narrow parameter of ripeness. If it's faintly green and underripe, I'll wait; if it's soft, overripe, or bordering on gnarly, into the freezer it goes. When enough freezer bananas pile up, it's time to make banana bread. This version is enriched with rice and orange juice.

1/2	cup orange juice
1/2	cup canola oil
1/2	cup buttermilk, skim milk, or rice milk
1	large egg plus 1 egg white
1	cup brown sugar
2	cups mashed ripe bananas (4 to 5 frozen and thawed bananas)
1	cup cooked short grain white rice or brown rice
2	cups unbleached all-purpose flour
1	teaspoon ground nutmeg
1	teaspoon ground allspice
1 1/2	teaspoons baking powder
1/2	teaspoon salt
1	cup diced walnuts, pecans or raisins

Preheat the oven to 350° F.

In a mixing bowl whisk together the juice, oil, milk, eggs, and sugar until creamy. Blend in the bananas and rice.

Mix the dry ingredients in a separate bowl. Gently fold the dry ingredients into the banana batter. Spoon the batter into two 8½ × 4½-inch greased loaf pans and bake for 50 minutes to 1 hour, until a toothpick inserted in the center comes out clean. Let the loaves cool on a rack for about 15 minutes before serving.

Yield: 2 small loaves

Rice Advice

If you really want to be decadent, frost the bread with Yogurt Cream Cheese Icing (page 207). Ooh la-la.

Horchata

Hearing that I was at work on a rice cookbook, two friends living in Panama sent this recipe via E-mail to my home. Horchata is a rice drink consumed throughout Central America and Mexico. It reflects the remarkable versatility of this worldly grain.

2	cups cooked white rice
2	cups lowfat milk or regular milk
2	to 3 tablespoons honey
1/4	teaspoon ground cinnamon
	Ice cubes

Combine all of the ingredients in a jar and shake vigorously. Refrigerate for 4 hours or overnight.

Strain the rice and reserve the liquid. Fill two glasses with ice and pour the milk over the top. Serve chilled. (For a rice shake, pour the rice and liquid into a blender and blend until creamy. Serve cold.)

Yield: 2 or 3 servings

Index

Hoppin' John, 93
Horchata, 210

Icing, yogurt cream cheese, 207
Indian rice pudding (kheer), 200
Indonesian fried rice, 182
Indonesian peanut sauce, 171
Island black beans and rice, 94–95
Italian garden risotto, 109
Italian tomato and bread bisque,
  40–41

Jamaican cook-up rice, 82–83
Jasmine rice with mixed leafy
  greens, 91
Jay's vegetable jambalaya,
  146–147
Jessica's black rice and pumpkin
  stew, 160–161

Kidney beans. see Red kidney beans
Kombu, about, 31

Lemongrass, about, 90
Lemony artichoke and rice, 58
Lentils
  herb-scented, rice salad and,
    60–61
  red, in dal, 170
  rice with, 88
  and vegetable curry, 144–145
Lettuce. see Greens

Mango sticky rice, 197
Maple-nut rice porridge, 180
Mediterranean herb and rice salad,
  50–51
Mexican corn and rice soup,
  38–39
Miami rice and avocado salad, 72
Middle Eastern rice with lentils, 88
Middle Eastern vermicelli pilaf,
  134–135
Mint, in blueberry rice
  pudding, 199
Miso rice soup, 30–31
Molasses, and apple rice bowl, 181

Muffins
  wild rice and pumpkin, 186
  zucchini carrot rice, 189
Mulligatawny. see Soups
Mushrooms
  and champagne and spinach
    risotto, 120–121
  and three grain soup, 46–47

Nasi goreng, 138–139
Native pumpkin and wild rice,
  26–27
Navy beans, and rice, 102–103
New Mexico red chile rice, 98–99
Nutty whole grain pilaf, 87

Orzo pilaf, 80

Paellas
  country garden, 152–153
  wild rice, with asparagus and
    corn, 154–155
Pancakes
  pumpkin-rice, 183
  spicy corn, 184–185
Pat soi, about, 131
Peach and apple chutney, 167
Peanut dressing, tofu and rice
  salad with, 66–67
Peas, curried rice and, 81
Pepperoncini
  about, 71
  and rice salad, 70–71
Peppers
  chili, roasting, 83
  chipotle, rice and beans with, 77
  Scotch bonnet, about, 83
Pesto
  with arugula basil, 174
  rice and zucchini salad, 68
  risotto, 141
  with spinach, 188
Pies, strawberry-rhubarb rice, 205
Pilaf. see also Pilau
  artichoke lover's, 140
  autumn, with roasted pumpkin,
    136–137

Pilaf, *continued*
basmati, and wild rice, 104–105
Greek spinach, 86
Middle Eastern vermicelli,
134–135
nutty whole grain pilaf, 87
orzo, 80
plantain, and wild rice, 96–97
stove top vegetable, 132
Pilau. *see also* Pilaf
pumpkin, 78
West Indian, 124–125
Piña colada rice pudding, 204
Pineapple fried rice, 187
Piquant creole sauce, 165
Plantains
roasted sweet, 176
and wild rice pilaf, 96–97
Polenta, riz cous, 190–191
Porridges
apple-molasses rice bowl, 181
maple-nut rice, 180
Potages. *see* Soups
Puddings
about, 195
arroz con leche, 201
banana-rum rice pudding, 198
black rice, 202
blueberry-mint rice
pudding, 199
chocolate mocha rice delight, 203
coconut sweet rice, 196
Indian rice (kheer), 200
mango sticky rice, 197
piña colada rice, 204
Puerto Rican vegetable asopao,
156–157
Pumpkins
pilau with, 78
and rice pancakes, 183
roasted, with pilaf, 136–137
stew, with black rice, 160–161
and wild rice muffins, 186

Quiche, asparagus rice, with
herbes de provence, 192–193
Quinoa and wild rice salad, 56–57

Raisin and carrot salad, with curried rice, 59
Raita, cucumber herb, 166
Rapini, in verdant risotto with
asparagus, 114–115
Red chiles and rice, 98–99
Red hot lava stir-fry, 148–149
Red kidney beans
creole, and rice, 100–101
and rice stew, 142–143
Red lentil dal, 170
Rhubarb, and strawberry rice
pie, 205
Rice
cooking, 3–5
glossary, 9–13
history, 7–8
nutritional value, 2–3
processing, 6
starch content, 7
storage, 6
Rice and sweet potato au
gratin, 150
Rice pot-au-feu, 44–45
Rice primavera salad, 53
Risi e bisi, 92
Risi minestrone, 24–25
Risotto
beet root, 116–117
champagne, mushroom, and
spinach, 120–121
cooking, 4
festive squash and sweet pea
with, 113
Italian garden, 109
pesto, 141
and squash, with escarole, 112
summer grill, 122–123
sun-dried tomato and white
bean, 118–119
sweet potato chowder and,
36–37
verdant, with asparagus and
rapini, 114–115
Riz cous
polenta, 190–191
and white bean salad, 69